D0396853

THE
OCTOPUS
AND THE
ORANGUTAN

ALSO BY EUGENE LINDEN

The Parrot's Lament
The Future in Plain Sight
Silent Partners
Affluence and Discontent
The Alms Race
Apes, Man, and Language

Linden, Eugene.
The octopus and the
orangutan : more true
c2002.
33305202792564
MI   12/11/02

OCTOPUS
AND THE
ORANGUTAN

More True Tales of
Animal Intrigue,
Intelligence, and Ingenuity

EUGENE LINDEN

SANTA CLARA COUNTY LIBRARY

3 3305 20279 2564

DUTTON
Published by the Penguin Group
Penguin Putnam Inc., 375 Hudson Street, New York, New York 10014, U.S.A.
Penguin Books Ltd, 80 Strand, London WC2R 0RL, England
Penguin Books Australia Ltd, Ringwood, Victoria, Australia
Penguin Books Canada Ltd, 10 Alcorn Avenue, Toronto, Ontario, Canada M4V 3B2
Penguin Books (N.Z.) Ltd, 182–190 Wairau Road, Auckland 10, New Zealand

Penguin Books Ltd, Registered Offices: Harmondsworth, Middlesex, England

Published by Dutton, a member of Penguin Putnam Inc.

First printing, August 2002
1   3   5   7   9   10   8   6   4   2

Copyright © Eugene Linden, 2002
All rights reserved

 REGISTERED TRADEMARK—MARCA REGISTRADA

LIBRARY OF CONGRESS CATALOGING-IN-PUBLICATION DATA HAS BEEN APPLIED FOR.

ISBN: 0-525-94661-6

Printed in the United States of America
Set in Palatino
Designed by Eve L. Kirch

Without limiting the rights under copyright reserved above, no part of this publication may be reproduced, stored in or introduced into a retrieval system, or transmitted, in any form, or by any means (electronic, mechanical, photocopying, recording, or otherwise), without the prior written permission of both the copyright owner and the above publisher of this book.

This book is printed on acid-free paper. ⊛

For Leon Levy, a true friend
throughout my career

CONTENTS

ACKNOWLEDGMENTS

D uring three decades of writing I have developed an even greater appreciation for those with special knowledge who are willing to share their expertise and experiences. I'd like to thank everybody, but *The Octopus and the Orangutan* builds upon reporting that dates back to the beginning of my career. In the interest of preserving the world's forests I will limit these acknowledgments to those who played a direct role in helping me with this book.

To get something right I often have to go back to a source several times, but where the nth call might understandably produce exasperation if not dread, all I have encountered has been civility and good humor. In this regard Richard Wrangham and his former Kibale colleague Carol Hooven have shown remarkable patience. I also am thankful for the hospitality and insights of Kathi Pieta, Kim Duffy, Donor Muhangyi, and Francis Mugurousi, who gave generously of their time during my visit to Kibale.

I am grateful also for the wonderful access provided by a number of zoos and aquariums around the country. At the Lincoln Park Zoo in Chicago, conversations with Eric Meyers, Andy Henderson, and Tracy Mott, among others, produced wonderful stories. A return visit to Seattle's Woodland Park

Zoo convinced me that I had not exhausted the rich vein of anecdotes in the memories of Andrew Antilla, Dana Wooster, and the other keepers. As always, the far-flung scientists, administrators, and curators of the Wildlife Conservation Society provided a wealth of material. Former director Bill Conway spoke eloquently about the role of zoos and the paradoxes of captivity; Diana Reiss, Louis Garibaldi, William Calvin, Jim Mullin, and JoAnne Basinger, all of whom are affiliated with the New York Aquarium, provided perspective and wonderful stories.

The book is the better for my conversations at the Dallas Zoo with Valerie Beardsley, Anita Schanberger, Bonnie Hendrickson, Jay Pratt, and Ray Shatwell, and with Brian Potvin at the Dallas Aquarium. Many thanks also to M.E. Sutton, who helped arrange my trip, and I cannot leave Texas without thanking John Forsythe, Nelson Herwig, and George Brandy for their wonderful stories about octopuses. Conversations and correspondence with Roger Hanlon (whose book *Cephalopod Behaviour* is perhaps the definitive work on octopuses and squid), Jean Baul, Jennifer Mather, and Roland Anderson helped me with additional stories and insights into the nature of these ancient and endlessly interesting creatures.

While still underwater, so to speak, I would like to acknowledge the help of Liz Thomas, Thad Lacinak, and Chuck Tomkins from SeaWorld in Orlando, Florida, for sharing orca lore. Laurie Merino helped me greatly to understand the workings of the dolphin brain.

My knowledge of the orangutan, the other animal in the title of this book, benefitted from my conversations with Willie Smits, Ann Russon, Lee Simmons, and Michael Soward. Though not mentioned in the title, the elephant looms large in this book, and I owe a debt to Harry Peachey, David Blasko, Ron Whitfield, Hugh Bailey, and Debbie Olson for sharing their stories.

Although I'm sure that it makes me rare, if not suspect, among writers, I have never regretted attending a scientific conference. For one thing, a conference on animal behavior often provides the best opportunity to speak with field biologists and other scientists who are otherwise very difficult to reach. Richard Connor, Randy Wells, Jack Bradbury, and Patricia Simonet are among the many scientists who graciously shared their insights.

I'd like to acknowledge the contribution of the people who have helped launch and publish this book. Esther Newberg continues to tolerate me in part because of her love of animals, and I am grateful for her representation. Both *The Parrot's Lament* and *The Octopus and the Orangutan* have had the great good luck of having Clare Ferraro as their champion. Carole Baron, Brian Tart, and their team supported this book from the very beginning. Mitch Hoffman and Stephanie Bowe have ably shepherded this book to print. This book also had the benefit of a critical reading by David Bjerklie, whose skeptical eye has saved me many times in the past.

Finally, thanks also go to my wife, Mary. Not many spouses would greet the news delivered on a Tuesday that their husband was heading off for Kenya and Uganda on Wednesday with such cheerful equanimity.

Chapter One

THE POWER
OF STORIES

As I sit here, poised to write an amusing story about ape intelligence, a squirrel peers down at me from a branch in the oak tree growing in my backyard outside my office window. My office sits behind my house, and looks out to the Hudson River. Squirrels seem to be having a great year. The oak has produced a bumper crop of acorns. The acorns suggest a hard winter, but the wide band on the wooly bear caterpillars I've encountered suggests a mild winter. So far, October and November have been among the warmest months ever recorded. Score one for the caterpillars, but we shall see.

Every day squirrels engage in pitched battles on the roof of the office. Every day I see breathtaking feats of squirrel acrobatics and tightrope walking. For the squirrels, the long telephone wire linking my neighbor's house to the pole on the street is a trade route, and they effortlessly scamper its length as though it were as wide as a boulevard. Where there isn't a convenient wire they improvise leaping from the ends of the high branches of the oak to the neighboring peach tree, grabbing a twig as though it were as sturdy as a hawser.

The squirrels are insultingly indifferent to stalking by our cats (who periodically mount futile big-game hunting expeditions), and find the squirrel-proofing defenses mounted around my neighbor's bird feeder (a smooth bell over a suspended feeder) a challenge rather than a barrier. Some of the birds—jays in particular—level the playing field with their own raids on squirrel acorn caches, and then the squirrels parry by raiding the jay's nests.

And so watching this circus just north of the Big Apple, I begin to wonder: Maybe I should be writing about squirrel intelligence. How can they be so flexible and innovative in their search for food, and not have some measure of intelligence? If a squirrel were scaled up to human size, its brain would be relatively large. Maybe there is something there.

This would be a departure from the typical investigation of animal intelligence. More likely, someone looking for signs of intelligence in the trees would seek out stories about monkeys or apes. In Tulsa, Oklahoma, there were news reports of a squirrel that would cross streets only when the "walk" sign was lit. If an ape did this, we might be more inclined to credit the notion that an animal could come to the conclusion that it was safer to cross the street when the funny looking white sign lit up (or, more likely, when people crossed the street). But a squirrel?

In shape, squirrels reprise the original design for primates such as smilodectes that emerged during the Paleocene about 60,000,000 years ago. Nature has come back to squirrel-like designs for primates several times since. Today, squirrel monkeys and ring tail macaques have squirrel-like characteristics. If something works, why change it? Looking out my window, it's easy to see how the squirrel with its bushy tail as a balance represents an optimum design for life in the trees.

So why did monkeys change from their original squirrel-like design? Why would they become smarter? Well, there is one very noticeable difference between monkeys and the early squirrel-like prosimians. The primates had hands configured for grasping. Could that simple difference have launched them on a path that eventually took their descendants out of the trees and into outer space?

And what about the squirrel? Somehow, squirrels developed bigger brains over time even as they maintained their basic form. Why did they get smarter, even as they maintained their secure niche in the swaying branches? Maybe they do have something to tell us about intelligence.

Ten years ago, I might never have connected my ruminations about squirrels to questions of animal intelligence. My prejudice, shared by many of the scientists who study these matters, was the natural inclination to look to big-brained mammals, particularly close relatives, for evidence of intelligence. It's easy to understand this bias, but I'm glad I'm getting over it. Sometimes the hardest thing to do is to recognize what is staring you in the face as you look out a window.

Or, as you stroll through a zoo.

Over the years, I have thought and written a lot about animal intelligence, but perhaps the most useful insight I've had has also been the most obvious: namely, that if animals can think at all, they probably do their best thinking when it serves their purposes. Once I walked through that door, an entirely new vista on animal minds materialized. It was this simple *aha!* moment that inspired me to write my last book, *The Parrot's Lament: And Other True Tales of Animal Intrigue, Intelligence, and Ingenuity*. Talking to zookeepers, trainers, veterinarians and others who deal with animals, I was inundated with stories about deception, trade and barter, games, cooperation, tool making and tool use, and other behaviors that suggested how animals think and what they think about.

These stories are not always easy to decode. Take, for instance, an encounter between great ape keeper Eric Meyers and a gorilla named Koundo some years ago. Koundo was then a 611-pound adult male living at the Lincoln Park zoo. One day Eric finished cleaning Koundo's habitat and left the area so that Koundo could be let back in. Once the gorilla was in his quarters, Eric, gathering his equipment, glanced back. Koundo was looking strangely at something on the floor. Eric looked down and saw that Koundo was staring at a fifty-dollar bill that had dropped out of Eric's pocket.

Eric offered a silent prayer that Koundo would simply forget the bill and move on, which would give Eric the opportunity to tempt him back out of the cage and retrieve the money. In retrospect, it was probably the wrong move for Eric to even think about the fifty-dollar bill, since the big gorilla might sense his anxiety and get curious. In any event, Eric watched in horror as Koundo bent over and picked it up.

Keepers do not make a lot of money, and Eric was not about to give up that bill without a fight. He leapt into action. Those who deal with great apes will regularly trade with their charges to get back objects that drop into their cages. It's an efficient way to retrieve lost objects without having to go to the trouble of getting the animals out of the area first.

Eric ran to the pantry and returned with a can of peaches, a Koundo favorite. With soothing words he offered Koundo some of the peaches in exchange for the fifty-dollar bill. Another bad move: The peaches alerted Koundo that he was holding something of value in his hand. Instead of returning the bill in exchange for peaches, Koundo did what gorillas, chimps and orangutans often do when they realize that they have something that their keepers want badly—he tore off a tiny piece of the bill and gave it to Eric, possibly with greedy thoughts of getting his hands on an entire case of peaches as he extended the transaction.

Eric could now envision getting his fifty-dollar bill back in five hundred pieces, so he decided to up the ante. There have been instances in which keepers have been able to convince animals that they will do better if they return something whole than they would by giving it back piece by piece. Eric decided to try this tack. He went back to the pantry and got every treat imaginable and laid them out like Emeril Lagasse presenting a Thanksgiving feast. Koundo looked in amazement at this cornucopia, then at the fifty dollars, and came to a decision. He popped the bill in his mouth and ate it.

I don't know quite what this story means, but I have no doubt that it reveals something about the workings of the gorilla mind. Maybe Koundo thought that if the exchange rate for fifty-dollar bills was the biggest feast he had ever seen in his life, they must be the best tasting treat ever invented. Or maybe, once he realized the bill's value, Koundo saw an opportunity to get back at Eric for some past slight. Maybe it represented something else entirely, but Koundo was clearly taking in the situation and coming to a decision—horrible for Eric, comical for us, and who knows what for Koundo.

This is a typical tale from a zoo. It's anecdotal, it shows some insight on the part of the gorilla (the idea of extending the money supply by returning the bill piece by piece), and it's ambiguous, but maybe it also offers an opportunity to see how animals think. These stories are the stuff of this book. Some are as ambiguous as the story about Koundo, some are clarion clear, and others are quite dramatic.

It took me many years to realize that these stories offered a worthy glimpse into animal minds. I was cautious simply because stories don't prove anything. Like most people who take this issue seriously, I wanted to see hard evidence and verifiable studies, particularly since concepts of human uniqueness are at issue, and the stakes are very high. Unfortunately, I'm still waiting. Studies have been done—scores of them—but they, too, almost always contain some maddening ambiguity, at least in the eyes of other scientists.

Frustration with the vituperative debate about the scientific studies ultimately led me back to wondering whether an obsession with controlled experiments and methods was actually obscuring our understanding of how animals think. The importance of this shift in perspective finally dawned on me when I heard about an orangutan named Fu Manchu's ingenious escapes from the Omaha Zoo. To briefly recap, Fu used a piece of wire to pick the lock on a door leading out of the orangutan enclosure at the zoo. He did this by pulling back on the metal flange on the door, creating a gap that allowed him to slide the wire up and trip the lock. Fu hid the wire between escapes and managed to pull off three breakouts before keepers figured out what was happening. After word about the escapes spread, Fu was made an honorary member of the American Association of Locksmiths.

Once I found multiple sources to verify this story, I began to realize what a trove it was. Fu's feats suggested that he could demonstrate a number of higher mental abilities, including tool making and tool use, and deception. Fu Manchu had sufficient problem-solving smarts to figure out how to unlock the latching mechanism and conceal his efforts from his keepers. Everything I have learned about Fu Manchu since the publication of *The Parrot's Lament* has only underscored the obvious: Animals do their best thinking when it serves their purposes. Indeed, the more I learn, the more extraordinary this ape seems.

Some months after the publication of *The Parrot's Lament*, I was talking with Lee Simmons, who knew Fu Manchu for many years when Simmons was curator of mammals at the Omaha Zoo. He was genuinely fond of the orangutan, noting that on at least four occasions Fu saved zookeepers from attacks by other orangs. Also, like many others who have dealt with orangutans, he saw their obvious intelligence. "I personally believe that orangutans are capable of abstract reasoning," Simmons remarked. "It's just difficult to test it in the animal because they can be so obstinate."

Simmons did not have to look far to find anecdotal evidence of orangutan intelligence since the animals were regularly demonstrating it in their attempts to escape. He noted several methods Fu employed before he resorted to picking locks with a piece of wire. One of the first was to unwind the wire in the chain link fence in his indoor quarters. Fu was strong enough to twist off a Sargent Lock, and sometimes he simply used brute strength to escape. When he was in temporary quarters he overpowered a number of padlocks and other locking mechanisms.

After many years at Omaha, Fu went down to the Gladys Porter Zoo in Brownsville, Texas. There he spent his later years helping to perpetuate the species by consorting with the zoo's female orangutans. "He had the retirement we all dream about," notes Simmons.

At one point during our conversation I asked him something that had been in the back of my mind since I first heard about the orangutan's escapes. Where, I wondered, had Fu gotten the piece of wire he used to pick the lock on the door that stood between him and the zoo beyond his enclosure?

When I first began checking up on the story of Fu Manchu's breakouts, I was preoccupied with the details of how he used the wire to trip the latch, and how he hid the wire between his lip and gum between escapes. This was enough to suggest a range of higher mental abilities, and it never occurred to me that the story would involve more than tool making, tool use, and deception.

But it did.

When not enjoying the outdoors, Fu and the other orangutans were housed in a series of cages separated by wire mesh. The orangutan colony included a female dubbed "Heavy Lamar" by the staff. Never a sylph, Heavy Lamar got so fat while housed with the other orangs that the keepers decided to put her on a diet. This entailed separating her from the other red apes. At the time of the escapes in which Fu used the wire, Heavy (I guess that would be her nickname) was being housed in a cage adjoining Fu's quarters. And she was ravenous.

As the keepers reconstructed the story, it looked for all the world as though Fu took advantage of the fat female's desperation by offering her monkey biscuits in exchange for a piece of wire in her cage—the wire that he eventually used as a lock pick. The evidence supporting this conclusion was circumstantial, but suggestive. For instance, before the escapes, keepers had seen Fu passing monkey biscuits to Heavy Lamar through the wire mesh. Only thinking back on the escapes did these off-hand observations take on any significance. After the escapes, they discovered that a wire leading to a lighting fixture in her cage had been broken off and stripped. Either by chance or design, that piece of wire ended up in Fu's possession.

The most routine explanation involves a combination of opportunism and mischief: Heavy Lamar stripped the wire out of mischief, and then came upon it later when she was scrambling around to find something that she might trade for a monkey biscuit. Fu took the wire in trade, and then, much later, Fu found a use for it.

Less likely, but still possible, is that Heavy Lamar begged Fu for monkey biscuits and he pointed to a piece of wire that she had earlier stripped from the fixture. In this version, it is possible that he pointed to the wire with no thought at that time that he would later use it to pick a lock.

From here, the possibilities become much more remote, but also much more interesting. Fu was a keen student of locks. Prior to picking the furnace-door lock, some of his earlier escapes had presented him with the opportunity to study the workings of door latches. It is conceivable that Fu knew what he would do with a piece of wire before he saw the wire either lying in Heavy Lamar's cage or in her hand. Then there is the most remote possibility of all: that Fu bribed Heavy Lamar to vandalize the lighting fixture so that he could get his hands on a piece of wire.

As long as we are considering remote possibilities, it is also conceivable that Heavy Lamar accidentally dropped the wire through the mesh, and that Fu simply kept it between his lip and gum because he couldn't think of a better place to put it, and that only when he pulled open the flange on the furnace door did he realize that he had a piece of wire that would enable him to reach the lock. This would be the explanation preferred by reductionists and skeptics of animal intelligence, because in this version, the only higher mental ability involved would be spontaneously improvised tool use—no mean feat, but certainly less impressive than the other possibilities.

Why do we care which explanation actually describes what happened? It is a good story no matter what the combination of motivations, but there is a world of difference in the implications of the various explanations. If it was a series of coincidences and accidents—the millionth monkey with a typewriter producing Hamlet—then the story would have more interest as an example of statistical improbabilities than it would as a case study of orangutan higher cognitive abilities. On the other hand, if Fu Manchu studied the lock and then hatched a scheme to bribe Heavy Lamar to vandalize the light fixture to procure the raw material he needed to fashion a tool so that he could escape without tipping his hand to his keepers . . . if this is what actually happened, then it would be game, set, and match for the orangutan team as far as demonstrations of animal awareness and higher mental abilities are concerned.

So, which explanation is the most plausible? Constrained by the principle of economy, most scientists would be forced to stick to some version of the reductionist explanation. One of the guiding assumptions of the study of cognition is Morgan's Canon, which cautions a scientist against ascribing a higher mental ability to an animal's behavior if the same behavior could be explained more simply as the result of serendipity or simple association.

While the rest of us should be respectful of scientific caution, we can be more judicious in the application of Morgan's Canon, which was probably never meant to be asserted as a law of the universe. According to scholars, Morgan himself later hedged his canon, noting that higher abilities could be inferred if they were supported by other compelling evidence. One could argue the case that the least plausible explanation for Fu's escape is that he got the wire by accident, used it only because he had it with him during the escape, then hid it between his lip and gum, not to conceal his tool from the keepers, but because he liked putting things in his mouth.

The tour de force aspect of this escape was the way all of the elements came together. There are numerous examples of orangutans demonstrating each of the components of the breakout. Fu may or may not have traded for the piece of wire, but trading is ubiquitous in captive situations involving a wide range of animals, although the great preponderance of trading involves animal-to-human transactions. Fu's use of the wire to pick the lock was an inspired choice, but orangutans have been discovered using a variety of tools other than keys to unlatch locking mechanisms. There are also numerous examples in which orangutans hid a tool in order to use it again. Thus the escape was an extraordinary linking of relatively ordinary orangutan behaviors in the zoo.

Why then should the most prudent interpretation of Fu's great escape be that it was the result of serendipity and coincidence? Isn't it just as probable that Fu was doing what he and other orangs have done many times before? Most scientists would agree with this, but then say that such stories still cannot be used as the basis for making assertions about orangutan intelligence, because anecdote is not science.

They are dead right, but this does not mean that stories of orang tool use and deception should be expunged from a behavioral scientist's mind when he or she ponders the question of orangutan intelligence. Stories of orangutan ingenuity can influence the investigation of animal intelligence in both positive and negative ways. There is the danger of reading too much into something an orangutan does because of the assumption that the animal is smart, but awareness of anecdotal evidence of intelligence can guide behavioral scientists toward interesting experiments. Rob Shumaker, who runs "Think Tank" at Washington's National Zoo, a long-term attempt to study orangutan intelligence, will freely admit that stories of orangutan problem-solving abilities influence the direction and design of many of his studies.

Marc Hauser, a professor of psychology and neuroscience at Harvard, and the author of *Wild Minds*, is about as hard-core an experimentalist as you can get. Still, he credits an unusual observation with stimulating his interest in the beliefs and desires of animals. As he tells the story in *Wild Minds*, the dominant male in a vervet monkey group in Kenya clobbered a female who was resisting the monkey's efforts to copulate. The female's screams caused other females to come running and give chase to the male. This continued until the male suddenly yelled out the alarm call that vervet monkeys use to signal the presence of a leopard. The posse chasing the male scrambled up into the trees, while the male who gave the call remained on the ground.

Hauser writes that he never saw a leopard, and the likelihood is that if one was present, the male would have fled to the trees, too. The implication is that the male purposely misled the chasing vervets to save himself from his outraged pursuers. On the other hand, Hauser notes that it is possible that the male simply made a mistake, and that until he knew more, it would be premature to make any assertions about the male's intent. Hauser sees such stories as a prompt for experiments.

That's as good as it gets when it comes to anecdote. Almost every scientist has a similar anecdote that inspired him or her, but few credit the stories of others. If you extracted a view of animal intelligence from a collection of these inspirational but unverifiable stories, I can guarantee that it would ascribe vastly more abilities than would be implied by the studies of the scientists who supplied the stories.

If we continue to assume no intelligence until it is incontrovertibly demonstrated, the comparative study of cognition will continue to be a free-fire zone in which scientists pick one another off each time someone raises their head to make the most modest assertion. While we wait for the scientific community to find some way to grapple with animal intelligence in a way that satisfies the need for scientific rigor without demanding ludicrous contortions from both animals and researchers, the rest of us can get some sense of whether there is intelligent life out there from credible stories of the ways in which animals use their wits in interactions with humans and each other.

A word on stories is in order. Many scientists look down on stories, or "case studies," as they are called when dressed up a bit and properly scrutinized. Stories, however, rather than the mathematical analysis of data, are how we understand the world. To his credit, Hauser recognizes this. "If you want to understand what an animal is thinking," he writes, ". . . then use these rare anecdotes to fuel your intuitions. These intuitions are essential for designing more careful observations and experiments."

What's true for psychologists is also true for other scientists. Even the hardest of the hard-nosed scientists, those sifting through impossibly large piles of data in cosmology and quantum mechanics, resort to metaphor and analogy when trying to explain or understand their data. So argued George Johnson in a marvelous essay in the *New York Times* on Christmas Day, 2001.

As Johnson noted, "explaining the strange in terms of the familiar—that is the essence of the scientific quest . . . Using metaphor and analogy, the tools of artists and poets, abstract patterns take on substance and become lodged more firmly in the mind." Ultimately, when we look at studies of animal behavior, we are looking for a familiar story that helps us understand what we are seeing.

Sometimes these stories run counter to received wisdom. Just as a scientist constructing a metaphor to make sense of his or her data must take care not to be misled by the power of the metaphor, so must these stories be kept in perspective. Those who traffic in compelling examples must guard against over-interpretation. Darwin's notion of evolution is a notable example of this. Evolution eventually provided the story that helped him understand how so many different finches could emerge in such close proximity when he began exploring the Galapagos Islands in 1831. As a story, evolution made sense to many other biologists of the era, but it ran counter to the common view of the world as the static creation of some divine power.

Darwin's great genius was to envision a theory that made sense of his observations, but there would be no theory without his observations. Instead of wondering why God would create such variety so close at hand, he opened his mind to see the obvious and came up with perhaps the single greatest idea of the last millennium.

Some of the stories in this book come from scientists, but they also come from zookeepers, trainers, veterinarians and others who deal with animals on a daily basis. The evidence, if that is what we can call it, lies in tales of escape, tool making and tool use, deception, games, trade and barter, and cooperation. All of these stories suggest that animals have mental as well as physical powers to draw on during their ongoing struggle to deal with nature, each other, and the looming presence of humans.

I began my previous book, *The Parrot's Lament*, wondering whether these tales of animal intrigue and ingenuity opened a new window on animal intelligence. I finished it, exhilarated and convinced that I had barely scratched the surface of what animals might tell us about the way they think. And so, let's cast another look at this fertile field. For one thing, since the publication of the book, I've learned significant new details about some of the central stories in *The Parrot's Lament*, and the cast of characters performing some of the more memorable feats has been expanding as well.

Orangutans, for instance, are not the only animals to show a gift for lock picking. At the other end of the phylogenetic scale, I came across the story of an octopus reputed to have picked the lock on its cage. If these and other octopus feats hold up to scrutiny, they pose a real challenge to the conventional wisdom about where we might expect to find intelligent behavior. Most scientists, for instance, assume that one prerequisite is a forebrain. We will take a closer look at the octopus in the next chapter.

Another lock picker is the elephant, a more natural choice perhaps because it has the largest brain of any land animal. On the other hand, the elephant does not have hands. This did not stop a female named Bandula at Marine World Africa USA. The incidents took place in the 1970s when the animal park was located in Redwood City, California, before it moved to its present location in Vallejo.

As was the case with Fu Manchu, the elephant used several methods to deal with locks and securing devices. In their nighttime quarters, the elephants wore leg shackles on chains, which permitted some movement, but not enough for fights and other encounters among the elephants. According to Ron Whitfield, now a keeper at the San Francisco Zoo, Bandula figured out how to break or unlock several of the devices used to secure the shackles. The most complicated of these was a

brommel hook, a latching device that closes when two oppos-
ing points are lined up and slid together. Bandula would play
with the brommel hook until the two points lined up and then
slide them apart. Once freed, on several occasions she would
then break or unlatch the shackles on the other elephants, and
the keepers would arrive in the morning to find the elephants
happily roaming, unshackled in their nighttime enclosure.

Diana Reiss, an expert on dolphin behavior now with the
Wildlife Conservation Society, worked at Marineworld in the
early 1980s. She and the other animal specialists would regularly get together and trade stories. She recalls one memorable
tale of elephant escape, in which the animals unscrewed the
bolts securing a big lock on the inside of the gate and then left.
In the morning they found the elephants outside the barn.

Worried about the dangers of free-roaming elephants, a
keeper hid out one night to see what was going on. To his as-
tonishment, the culprits turned out not to be human vandals,
but the elephants themselves. Once everyone had left for the
night, the female would walk up to the gate, look around to
make sure the coast was clear, and then use the highly manip-
ulable nubs at the end of her trunk (which are as dexterous as
fingers) to grab the bolts on the lock and twist them off. Then
she simply opened the gate and she and her pals went back
outside into their paddock.

As was the case with Fu Manchu, there was an element of
deception in this jailbreak, as evidenced by the female elephant's looking around. She not only knew how to escape, she
also seemed to know that she needed to be clandestine if she
was to succeed. Like Fu Manchu, she seemed to factor the
knowledge state of her keepers into her plans, recognizing that
if they were aware of her plans they could foil them.

There are stories of other animals looking around before attempting an escape or theft, and they involve animals that
range from raccoon to dolphin. If these animals were aware of

the knowledge of their keepers, they could be said to have a theory of mind, one of the hallmarks of consciousness. On the other hand, the reductionist explanation would be that the animals made some simple association between the presence of humans and consistently thwarted plans.

Apart from new material on the species and categories of *The Parrot's Lament*, there are new animals, like the octopus, the crow, and even the penguin, that merit a look, as well as a broader range of behaviors that provide glimpses into the animal mind. Some new stories are astonishing—animals using weapons, using bait, and building elaborate tools—and some of the most astonishing new stories come from wild parts of the most remote corners of the globe.

I will also push deeper into some of the bedeviling conundrums of the study of intelligence, which perpetually promises answers that always seem to lie just over the horizon. The promise that we will crack the nature of intelligence and be able to replicate it is an idea that has become embedded in popular culture as well. The year 2001 came and went without the advent of HAL, the intelligent computer of Stanley Kubrick's 1968 film. Computers remain idiot savants, although give them a task for an idiot savant, such as beating Garry Kasparov in chess, and they prove quite formidable. (While overestimating advances in computation and space travel, the makers of *2001* completely underestimated advances in communications, but that's typical of science fiction, which provides more of an image of the time during which it was created than of the future.)

Today, prominent cybergurus, such as internet pioneer Bill Joy, fear that a robot takeover may lie in the future. We will see. If building intelligent machines depends on humanity figuring out the nature of intelligence, I would argue that we have nothing to worry about. Fifty years from now, scientists will still be squabbling over these questions, and I would not at all be surprised if some entirely new theory of intelligence emerged. On the other hand, it remains conceivable that we might produce machines that replicate intelligent behavior without even knowing what intelligence is.

In any event, the sciences that study intelligence and consciousness still swirl with new studies and controversy. Many of the stories that will unfold offer a perspective on this debate, and carry with them their own implications about the nature of intelligence. There is no agreement about the definition of this signal ability—there is even longstanding debate about whether intelligence is one ability or an ensemble of many. When you think about it, this is astonishing in itself, since the planet's greatest minds have been struggling to understand intelligence since antiquity. Still, there is plenty of lively thinking, as well as a flood of new evidence about what is going on in the brain when we or other species think, communicate, and dream.

I enter this new book with the humility of someone who has watched the maddening question of the nature and origins of intelligence embitter some of the finest scientific minds around. I am neither a naturalist nor a behavioral psychologist, but I have been exploring this question for a long time. Moreover, given the harsh treatment meted out to those scientists who venture beyond the conservative conventional wisdom of the various disciplines concerned with animal intelligence, having an outsider's perspective is not such a bad thing.

Chapter Two

THE RIDDLE OF THE OCTOPUS

Unlikely Minds

Consider the octopus, one of the most enduring and successful designs nature ever perfected. While humans might trace our immediate line back some 200,000 years, the ancestry of our hominid forebears another 5 to 8 million years, and our primate roots as much as 35 million years, the modern octopus may have roots in the Devonian period over 370 million years ago. It's hard to tell how old the octopus line really is since the boneless creature fossilizes terribly. Still, there is evidence that its ancestors predate mammals, fish, and even woody trees.

The basic octopus design is little changed since the Jurassic period. Earlier forms nicely survived the great extinctions of the end of the Permian period 245 million years ago, which wiped out 96 percent of all marine species, and the end of the Cretaceous period 65 million years ago, which killed off 85 percent of Earth's living biota. Over the eons they have invaded and adapted to practically every marine region, from coral gardens to the Arctic and from tidal pools at the edge of the sea to the deep abyss 7,000 meters below the surface. Even today, they are invading new niches already occupied by formidable competitors, such as bony fishes. There are over 250 species today, and there may never have been more diversity in octopuses than there is today. Clearly, the octopus is an evolutionary success story.

Octopuses are part of the class of sea life called Cephalopoda (Latin for "head foot") which, apart from squid, include nautilus and cuttlefish. Octopuses are mollusks and thus also number bivalves such as clams and oysters among their relatives, as well as gastropods such as snails. Along their long evolutionary path they lost the characteristic shell of other mollusks, and developed their extraordinarily dexterous arms equipped with the suckers that allow them to crawl up a sheer glass or pick up anything that captures their fancy.

They also developed an extraordinary array of weapons and defenses, perhaps the most dazzling of which is their so-called chromatophore system, which consists of specialized pigment cells that, controlled by muscles, mix different colors until a desired effect is achieved. Octopuses can change appearance as much as twenty times a minute. Humans can relate to some of the basic color reactions of the octopus, since it often turns white with fear and red with anger. It's unclear whether they turn green with envy.

John Forsythe, a biologist with twenty-five years experience studying octopuses in the wild and in the lab at the Marine Biomedical Institute in Galveston, Texas, did a study of this camouflage. The animal's ability to change its appearance beggars any stealth technology devised by humans. Forsythe's work found that the octopus deployed its camouflage about 50 percent of the time, usually to confuse potential predators by showing its enemies many different search images. Imagine the poor barracuda looking down: "Hmmm, there's a flounder, no wait, it's a lion fish, egad, it's a sea snake . . . fuggedaboudit!"

It's not just colors that the octopus can change. Through muscle control it can even adjust the texture of its skin from frilly to smooth depending on what disguise the animal wants to assume. As one boneless set of muscles, the octopus can also distend its body to squeeze through astonishingly small openings. The only limitation is the width of its beak and brain case, which it cannot compress and which are about the width of its eye. In the laboratory researchers have watched an octopus squeeze itself through a 1.5-inch-wide clear pipe, assuming a wormlike shape in the process, to get to another tank holding a tasty crab.

Nelson Herwig, who designed the Houston Aquarium and has run it since 1978, notes that on one occasion the staff thought that one of the aquarium's giant Pacific octopuses had escaped, since the animal was nowhere to be found in its tank. Closer examination revealed that this octopus had somehow crawled through a drain pipe and was living, happy as a clam (so to speak), underneath the filter plate in the tank. Here was an animal that could stretch ten feet from tentacle to tentacle, and yet could slither through a two-inch-wide pipe. They had to dismantle the tank to retrieve the animal who, according to Herwig, was quite content in his little hideout.

While these powers are worthy of *Ripley's,* there is no reason for the octopus to be aware of them. With tens of millions of generations to play with, it is not surprising that nature would gradually equip the octopus with a nervous system that can send messages that configure the incredible color palette in the octopus's skin into a mimicry of some of the sea's least appetizing denizens. The genius of the octopus's coloration is the genius of evolution.

In nature, the solution might be ingenious, but the animal itself might be a dullard. Dim-wittedness is the one thing that unites nature's most durable creatures, from sea turtles to jellyfish to paddlefish to nematodes. Short-lived prolific bugs tend to weather crises, as do some deepwater creatures, well insulated from events above, for instance, but there is little correlation between brain size and a species' long-term survival.

Nature is loath to tamper with success, and it is loath to

lay on brains where they are not needed. How and why brains develop in some animals and not in others is a mystery. The random mutations that increase brain size are probably ubiquitous, meaning that it is reasonable to expect that virtually every animal alive today has ancestors that produced brainier offspring which in turn had the chance to be fruitful and multiply. But the evidence is that with very few exceptions, evolutionary experiments to increase brain power have not taken. During the march of evolution, many animals have gotten smarter in the way we define it, but not much smarter. The likelihood is that nature has had more failures than successes when it comes to increasing brain size (and in evolutionary terms, the jury is still out on whether the human experiment will ultimately be a success or failure, but more about that later).

It's also possible that brains can get smaller when they are not needed. This makes evolutionary sense, since the brain diverts blood that would otherwise make an animal stronger and faster. An obvious candidate for this regression might be river dolphins, who have found a pretty cozy niche in the rich waters of the Amazon and other major rivers. There they have an abundant but limited food supply and are safe from sharks, orcas, and other dolphin-eating terrors of the deep. Typically, they have much smaller brains than their pelagic relatives in the oceans. Laurie Merino, of Emory University, and her colleague Mark Ewan, of Michigan's Cranbrook Institute, are currently searching through the fossil record to determine whether river dolphin brains have shrunk or simply not gotten larger (one piece of evidence suggesting shrinkage is that river dolphins have gradually lost visual acuity and thus have less call on visual processing capacity in the brain).

Where animals do have bigger brains, the immediate reason for an increase in size may have nothing to do with the need to read Proust. The dolphin, a mammal, might have evolved into a creature with a brain like a cow's or hippo's had it not returned to the sea (fifty-million-year old fossils of early whales recently found in Pakistan suggest that whales and hippos share a common ancestor). Dolphins still retain behavioral relics from their ungulate roots in such behaviors as head-to-head confrontational stances. Part of the dolphin's large brain may have evolved to enable the processing of high-frequency acoustic information, and maybe the animal's obvious intelligence comes as an adjunct to these mundane utilitarian functions. Similar pressures did not produce large brains in bats, however, another mammal that abandoned life on land, in this case to make its life in the skies rather than the oceans.

As for the octopus, there are various theories as to why this invertebrate has a relatively large brain. In a 1972 paper, Andrew Packard argued that octopus brain growth was a response to the arrival of the teleost fishes in the Devonian period. Until predators such as grouper, barracuda, snappers, and striped bass came along, the cephalopods pretty much ruled the seas. From that time forth, however, octopuses and squid began putting some distance between themselves and their hard-shelled relatives in terms of brainpower.

Indeed, some of the octopus's close relatives have survived to the present without ever developing a head, much less a brain. For whatever reasons, the octopus embarked on a different path. A giant Pacific octopus brain is about the size of three walnuts (with the equivalent of another few walnuts in neurons outside the brain, in its arms). While but a tiny fraction of the size of a human brain, the octopus's brain still compares favorably with most fish and some birds. What is perhaps more meaningful, the octopus has developed the largest brain of any invertebrate. The key part of that sentence, however, is that little phrase "of any invertebrate." Talking about a large-brained invertebrate is like referring to the world's swiftest snail. Octopuses can learn by trial and error and remember what works, but the cephalopods simply don't have many of the brain structures we associate with intelligence.

Which brings us to the riddle of the octopus. Ask one thousand scientists which animals would be at the top of their list as most likely to demonstrate intelligence, and not one of them will mention the octopus. On paper, the squirrels outside my window look far more promising than the octopus. Chimps, orangutans, bonobos, and gorillas will be on everybody's list because they are big-brained and close relatives of humans. Dolphins and whales will be on the list, too, because they, too, have big, highly developed brains and complicated social structures—one of the factors that supposedly play a crucial role in the evolution of the human brain. Elephants, too, have big brains and elaborate social structures, so the scientist casting a wide net might include elephants. Those willing to court a raised eyebrow among their colleagues might go as far as considering parrots, crows, wolves, or even sea lions, but probably not a mollusk.

While those who champion the octopus quickly (and a mite defensively) will tell you that the animal has a lot of neurons, it really does not have a brain in the sense that we do. Being an invertebrate, it doesn't even have a backbone. Why would anybody look for intelligence in a species that numbers the clam among its distant relatives? The difficulties of imagining an intelligent mollusk are embodied in octopus websites, many of which alternate stories of octopus intelligence with recipes for cooking the animal.

It gets worse. Behavioral scientists argue that social complexity correlates strongly with the evolution of higher mental abilities. Far from being social, the octopus is solitary. If one encounters another cephalopod, it is as likely to try to eat it as greet it.

Then there is the question of life span. Long-lived animals are more likely to be intelligent, under the reasoning that the cost/benefit analysis of natural selection is unlikely to invest the time in developing and programming intelligent behavior in a creature unless the animal is likely to live long enough for that investment to pay off. By contrast, many octopuses live little more than a year, some as little as six months, and the longest-lived species, the 110-pound giant Pacific octopus (the largest ever weighed six hundred pounds and spanned thirty-one feet), lasts at most five years before it dies.

Other clues for signs of intelligence include a protracted childhood and adolescence (so that the brain can grow and the animal can learn the rules of the game; most great apes, humans included, do not function as adults until their teens), and a long life after menopause (an indication that the animal contributes knowledge vital to the welfare of the species after its reproductive life is over). The octopus fails these tests as well. Most never meet their mother since she dies right after the eggs are hatched, and adolescence passes in the blink of an eye for these short-lived animals. There are other guides that scientists use to narrow their search for intelligent species, and the octopus fails them all—except for one, which I will get to in a moment. Screened for anatomy, social structure, and phylogenetic history, the octopus should be dumber than a sackful of hammers.

But it is not. If we put aside expectations and simply look at some of the things an octopus can do, a different picture emerges. John Forsythe, for instance, ran a series of experiments to see how well an octopus could negotiate a maze. He built a complicated vertical maze in which he put an octopus on one side of a glass wall and a tasty crab on the other. The octopus very quickly figured out how to climb the wall and get the crab.

So, Forsythe started making things more difficult. First he extended the wall with an opaque board so that the octopus could not maintain visual contact with its prey. Then he added a top, so that the octopus, while out of sight of its prey, first had to head away from the crab in order to gain its prize. Forsythe says that there was no water movement, so he is sure that the octopus was not getting sensory signals about the location of the crab, and that even if there had been such signals, the octopus still would have had to head in the opposite direction in order to get to the crustacean.

Forsythe was amazed at the results. He says that he frankly expected it not to work, but the octopus proved to be a whiz at learning the ins and outs of the maze. The animal had to somehow keep track of the fact that the crab was, as Forsythe put it, "over here and down there," even as it went the opposite direction and up. As a cautionary note, Forsythe says that the octopus would probably not have been able to figure it out if presented with the most complicated form of the maze at first. "It had to remember routes, and build a new route map as it went on," says Forsythe, "but it usually did this very quickly."

Forsythe was impressed by these abilities, but regards them as an extension of what octopuses regularly do in the wild, not an entirely new behavior. The animal is a predator, well equipped to seek out and snare prey that typically will hide in hard-to-get-at places. As the animal explores an area, its tentacles probe every crevice looking for a potential snack. What looks like intelligent behavior might simply be the application of genetically encoded search rules, efficiently applied.

But every now and then the octopus does something that leaves scientists scratching their heads. What does it say about octopuses that they have staged escapes very similar to the orangutan Fu Manchu's jailbreak from the Omaha Zoo?

In 1964, at the Monaco facility of the late undersea explorer Jacques Cousteau, workers began to notice that the new specimens they were bringing in during the day were disappearing at night. There was no sign of a break-in, and the mysterious disappearances continued for several days, until a Mediterranean octopus was discovered to be the culprit. The octopus had been sneaking out of its cage at night, climbing into the collection cages, and then returning, looking as innocent as an octopus can look in its own cage.

Since this episode came to light in Cousteau's writings and in Frank Lane's book, *The Kingdom of the Octopus*, there have been literally dozens of stories of similar octopus thefts: octopuses stealing lobsters at Scripps Institution of Oceanography and the Seattle Aquarium, and crabs and fish elsewhere. Indeed, the stories are so prevalent that many scientists assume that these tales are the aquatic version of an urban legend, particularly since it is a lot easier to find secondhand retellings than firsthand accounts of such incidents.

John Forsythe, for instance, is one of the skeptics. He accepts that something like this might happen if it did not involve a lot of climbing and if the neighboring tank was quite close by. Octopuses are known to crawl out of water when they move between tide pools, so it is not beyond the octopus's behavioral repertoire for the animal to take the risk of crossing dry land. On the other hand, Forsythe says that they usually completely "freak out" when they find themselves out of the water, with their arms going in every direction. (Despite his scientific caution, Forsythe remains in awe of octopus abilities, noting that it is one of the very few invertebrates that can go "head to head" with vertebrates.)

Others have no doubts that the octopus skullduggery is real. Louis Garibaldi, the director of the New York Aquarium, is a much-traveled curator and director, having worked at the Steinhardt Aquarium in San Francisco, the National Aquarium in Washington D.C., and the New England Aquarium, among other facilities. He says that at the Steinhardt Aquarium, the octopuses would crawl out and steal crabs and then return to their tank. Garibaldi says that sometimes the octopuses did not make it back (if their gills are out of water too long they start to dry out and lose permeability), and the curators would occasionally find dead octopuses on the floor between the tanks in the morning.

To foil octopus escapes, Garibaldi simply put Astroturf on the tank walls above the water line and made sure that the top of the tank was higher than an octopus could reach. The animals hate Astroturf because their tentacles cannot get suction on the material and because of its prickly feel. Nelson Herwig tried that, only to discover that the giant Pacific octopuses figured out a way to reach over the Astroturf and haul themselves out. One night at 2:30 A.M., Herwig remembers getting a call from a night watchman who had found a forty-pound octopus in the middle of the floor. The watchman had picked up the animal—something not every night watchman would do— and put it in the nearest tank. Unfortunately, the nearest tank was for warm-water fish, and the octopus, which lives in very cold waters in the northern Pacific, ultimately died of the shock.

Herwig remembers another occasion when he was bringing a group of docents through the Houston facility to show them the octopuses. He failed to notice a supervisor trying to get his attention. Not seeing the octopus in the tank, he assumed the cephalopod was hiding and the group moved on. George Brandy, the supervisor who had been waving, told Herwig later that he had been trying to get his attention because an octopus had escaped and was hiding in the drainage channel on the floor.

The animal had escaped in the brief, two-minute period when the keepers had the tank lid open while they were cleaning the exhibit. Brandy recalls that once they realized the octopus was gone, they began frantically looking for the animal. This is what they were doing when Herwig arrived with the donors. Once the guests arrived, all the keepers could do was pretend that all was well, and hope that the octopus, who was happily exploring the floor around the drainage with a tentacle, did not take it into his mind to grab one of the ladies by the ankle.

ᵉ Herwig laughs at the havoc that might have occurred if the octopus had snaked a tentacle around a Houston matron's leg, but the woman would not have been in danger. The animals are one big muscle and are tremendously strong, says Herwig, but they become quite docile and gentle when picked up by people. On the other hand, Herwig says that if hungry, one particular octopus—which would ordinarily play with people very amicably—would grab and not let go unless fed. This same octopus had another trick to let his keeper know when he was hungry. If the keeper was out of reach, he would jet a gallon of icy cold water at the keeper when he wanted to be fed. (George Brandy recalls that another octopus had a habit of drenching red-haired women who passed his exhibit.)ᵉ

Octopuses, like orangutans, seem to have a good deal of interest in locking mechanisms. George Brandy recalls that in the early 1980s, the octopuses were kept in tanks with lids, latched shut with sliding bolts. To facilitate the exchange of oxygen, the plastic lids were perforated with holes that were too small to permit an octopus to escape, but, apparently, large enough for them to snake through a bit of a tentacle. Brandy reached this conclusion because the keepers kept returning to find the lids in place, but the sliding bolt locks opened. While this was never observed, Brandy surmises that they managed to get enough of a tentacle through to slide back the latch, permitting them to lift the lid.

Octopus escapes are wonderful stories, but they may not necessarily indicate intelligence. It's amazing what a persistent animal can accomplish through simple trial and error. Not that much is known about the communication between the animal's brain and its tentacles. Martin Wells of Cambridge University in England concluded as the result of some studies that the octopus may not "know" where the ends of its arms are. Each of the eight octopus arms may be configured to constantly and autonomously explore. When it finds something interesting, perhaps the octopus brain then takes charge to coordinate a response.

What is known is that the tentacle is a wonderfully flexible instrument with an extraordinary variety of uses. Roger Hanlon, a biologist at the Marine Biological Laboratory in Woods Hole, Massachusetts, has spent much of his life studying octopuses in the wild, and is the co-author with John Messenger of *Cephalopod Behaviour*, regarded as the definitive book on the subject. He notes that the octopus arm is what is called a "muscular hydrostat." Like the human tongue and the elephant trunk, its flexibility derives from the coordinated contraction and relaxation of various muscles. While the human arm is a series of hinge joints that we move and rotate through control of muscles like the triceps and biceps, the octopus has four kinds of muscles in each arm and probably uses all of them to control movements. The animal can control the suction of the suckers on its tentacles as well, applying gentle suction where appropriate or quite powerful suction if it wants to do something like pull itself through a two-inch drain pipe.

This requires a lot of brain capacity, and nature has come up with an ingenious solution. Some three-fifths of the animal's neurons are outside of its brain, principally in its arms. Each of the animal's arms has as many as two hundred suckers and each of the suckers is supported by ten thousand neurons. It's as though each arm has a separate brain. Some scientists think that it is possible to teach one octopus arm a behavior that another arm does not know. There are also stories of octopus arms, detached from the body, that still perform functions such as passing food up suckers.

At least some measure of octopus "intelligence" seems to be distributed. Curiously, what nature designed for the octopus millions of years ago has been adopted by computer designers in recent decades. Largely unaware of the fact that nature got there first, pioneering computer engineers started exploring the problem of distributed intelligence in the 1980s in work focused on designing computer systems and robots.

Until then, computer science had largely concentrated on building ever faster central processors so that one machine could handle all computations and tasks. Then a number of thinkers began exploring an entirely different model for computer design. Instead of looking at process, they shifted focus to the outcome. If a robot can efficiently clean up a room, no one is going to care how it figured out how to do its job. Engineers discovered that a lot of small processors doing specific tasks in different parts of a robot or distributed in a network could actually produce better results than an IBM supercomputer crunching numbers at warp speed. In the years since, distributed processing has become the paradigm in both problem solving and robotics. In essence, computer engineers have gravitated to an approach to solving problems that nature seemed to already have chosen in its tinkerings that resulted in the octopus.

And so, inevitably, the field of robotics has discovered the octopus itself. Last year Hanlon organized a workshop at the Marine Biological Laboratory in which he brought together engineers, biologists, biomechanical experts and computer modelers to see whether it might be possible to create a biomimetic arm based on the octopus. Hanlon says they are not very far along. It stands to reason that it might take a bit of time to recreate something mechanically that nature perfected over many millions of years.

But what does distributed intelligence have to do with intelligence? The British mathematician and code breaker Alan Turing spent some time pondering the possibility of developing a thinking machine. He developed a simple test to determine whether a robot or computer exhibited intelligence. If a questioner could not determine whether the answers to a series of questions he posed came from a machine or a human, then Turing claimed that the machine could be said to be intelligent. (This idea loses a lot of its sex appeal when pondered for any length of time; the answer to the question of whether an unidentified object being questioned was human or machine would more likely be revealed in the back and forth of conversation—often in ways far removed from questions relating to intelligence—than in the content of the answers. I will have more to say about this in later chapters.)

No one is ever going to confuse an octopus for a human, but the notion of distributed intelligence raises an interesting question: Is something intelligent if what we are observing is in part the result of distributed neurons acting together, rather than one centralized brain? Robotics designers have gotten robots to play soccer as a team sport by installing simple rules that ask the robot to remember and repeat what it was doing in circumstances that were advantageous to scoring a goal or playing defense. Using this system, the designers got the simple robots to gradually learn various positions on the team. It is not a stretch to imagine that over time, more sophisticated robots could gradually become competent in a host of behaviors, going through the day performing tasks as a human would, without in any way being aware of what they were doing (this is pretty close to how strict behaviorist psychologists describe human learning, by the way). Would this robot be aware?

Without becoming mired in various theories of how the brain works, one point is worth raising. The brain itself, though unified in one place, pools and interprets the input of centers distributed throughout our gray matter that collect and redirect sensory information. Could these pooling and interpretive functions still develop if some neurons were a few centimeters apart rather than separated by a couple of millimeters? The fact of the matter is that we don't know where awareness lies, except that in humans it seems to reside in the forebrain.

It is nothing but healthy that the octopus forces us to consider such issues as distributed intelligence, the importance of dexterity and vision in developing intelligence, and whether different brains might utilize different areas, organization, or even chemistry to increase problem-solving abilities. These questions arise because the octopus does interesting things. Let's look now at some of the stories that caught the attention of octopus observers.

Chapter Three

OCTOPUS DERISION, OCTOPUS DECISIONS

*Why the Octopus Has a
Brain Instead of a Shell*

Intelligent outcomes do not imply intelligent behavior. Over time, nature can work out designs that are more efficient, more elegant, more appropriate, more *intelligent* than anything devised by man. Bat sonar and wing design, for instance, permit aerobatics far beyond the capacity of present-day engineering. So is the miniaturization in the design of the ordinary housefly, according to neuroanatomists, but neither the fly nor the bat need be intelligent. Still, we can't yet write off the octopus as one of nature's wind-up toys that mimics intelligent behavior.

For one thing, octopuses keep doing things that wind-up toys don't do. And while critics come up with a reductionist explanation for these apparant flashes of insight, these examples always seem to leave a lingering sense of wonder even in the minds of hard-nosed skeptics. Such was the case with one experiment led by Graziano C. Fiorito of the Zoological Station of Naples, Italy.

His study seemed to suggest that octopuses are capable of observational learning, something regularly observed in primates where the young often learn by watching their mothers and others, but completely unexpected in a mollusk, which spends no time with its mother or peers at all. In this instance, the scientists used rewards and punishments to teach several captive octopuses to choose a red ball rather than a white one. The experimenters purposely conducted this teaching in view of other octopuses. When these observing octopuses were allowed to choose between red and white balls, they overwhelmingly chose the red ones.

This was not a perfect experiment (what is!). Jean Baul, a biologist specializing in octopus behavior at Millersville University in Pennsylvania, notes that a number of rebuttals of Fiorito's work made the point that the observing octopus had its attention drawn to the octopus being trained. Roger Hanlon argues that what Fiorito saw as one octopus learning from another might have been a more generalized form of observational learning. For instance, rather than saying, "Gee, the octopus that chooses the red ball gets a reward," it might have been unconcerned with octopus behavior but interested in a correlation between the red ball and food. This would not fit the strict definition of observational learning that psychologists use (in which an animal must learn by watching another of its same species), but might still qualify as a type of observational learning.

However, even those like Hanlon and Baul, who rank themselves among the skeptics about octopus intelligence, sometimes see anecdotal evidence that the cephalopod has something going on upstairs. Octopuses are sticklers for fresh food, and one day Jean remembers that she was feeding a group of California mud flat octopuses (*binaculoides*) a meal of squid and shrimp. The food was a little past its peak of freshness. She would give each animal its first portion of food, and then go back to the beginning of the line of tanks to give them a second serving. When she got back to the first tank, a female octopus was waiting at the front of the tank. At this point, Jean says the octopus made eye contact with her while taking the piece of shrimp in one of her tentacles. Maintaining eye contact all the while, she then crawled over to the drain at the bottom of the tank and unceremoniously shoved the offending meal into the opening, where it was carried away. What makes the story so funny and arresting is the eye contact and the dexterity that enabled the animal to hold the spoiled shrimp while she slithered across the bottom of the tank. There is something about eye signals and manual dexterity that suggests intelligent behavior.

In fact, many of the animals that show signs of intelligence have fine motor control of their hands or an equivalent. Exceptions, such as the elephant or the dolphin, have other means of satisfying their curiosity. The tip of an African elephant's trunk has two fingers, about half the length of a human finger, that the animal can use with great precision. David Blasko, the chief of animal operations for Marine World Africa USA in Vallejo, California, says that an elephant can grab and unscrew a ⅜-inch hexagonal bolt, and that elephants at his facility will regularly use their trunks to turn on a faucet when they want a drink of water, a trick they picked up through observation. Dolphins don't have hands (although their acoustic imaging capabilities can more than satisfy dolphin inquisitiveness—dolphins regularly scan their trainers with sonograms and some appear to know when female trainers are pregnant before the women themselves).

In a broad sense, the octopus may have other similarities with humans that help explain its relative advantage in brainpower over its hard-shelled cousins. Both the octopus and *Homo sapiens* are creatures that in effect traded armor for brains. Physically, the strongest human could not hold his own with a half-grown chimp, gorilla or orangutan. Our defenses derive from the coordinated application of human numbers and brains and in the weapons we make. The fact that we survived and prospered has ratified these choices by natural selection.

Similarly, as the octopus's ancestors evolved, the gains from mobility, flexibility, and keener senses must have offset the loss of a protective carapace. Lou Garibaldi of the New York Aquarium says that we can see these trade-offs in the evolution of the vision of various mollusks. The scallop has a hard shell and can get by with a sensory apparatus that distinguishes changes in light as a shadow (meaning a predator) passes over it, signaling the scallop to close the gates. In the same family are gastropods, which, compared to a scallop, are highly mobile. Snails developed eye stalks, which allowed some freedom of movement. Without a shell and much more mobile, the octopus developed an eye that rivals our own in its ability to distinguish fine details when looking for food on the bottom or maintaining vigilance against predators. The development of its eyes was accompanied by the development of two large orbital lobes in the octopus's central nervous system.

Hanlon notes that as a soft-bodied creature without spines or other active forms of retaliation, the octopus may depend more on learning than its well-armored relatives. There are occasional suggestions that octopuses miss their shell. During a stint at the New England Aquarium, Lou Garibaldi came across octopuses that lived on the muddy bottom of the waters off New England. These octopuses apparently feel a little insecure in this exposed environment, and some will grab a half clam shell and hold it over themselves like a helmet; in effect, notes Garibaldi, they are saying, "I want to be a mollusk."

Octopuses may not be social, but a number of scientists claim that they are capable of recognizing different people. Jennifer Mather, an octopus specialist in the department of psychology and neuroscience at the University of Lethbridge in Canada, has done field work showing that octopuses are often followed by fish looking to grab the odd scrap of food dropped by the predators. Mather suggests that octopuses may be able to distinguish between friendly and unfriendly fish, and if they can do that, it is possible that they can distinguish between the people they encounter.

Mather is less shy about pushing the case of octopus intelligence than many of her colleagues. She believes that octopuses do recognize different people, noting that they very quickly figure out who is feeding them. One way an octopus expresses its displeasure is to jet water. Mather says that one time she pressed down on the lid of a tank to prevent an octopus—*Octopus vulgaris*—from escaping. For the next few days, every time Mather passed this particular tank, she would be greeted by a jet of water.

The animal's water jet seems to be a multi-purpose tool. The muscles that enable it to jet water primarily help respiration and the elimination of wastes, but the octopus uses this ability in a variety of ways. Mather has observed octopuses jet water in what looked like an effort to clean their den. The octopus will gather up rocks and detritus in the den and then blast them away. She has also documented octopuses using their water jets to repel fish that scavenge the waste piles that build outside the octopuses' den.

Using water as a tool is one thing, but Mather goes further and argues that the animal has the capacity for play. She has watched an octopus repetitively retrieve an empty, floating pill bottle that was pushed toward her by a water inlet jet and push it back towards the jet, whereupon the water stream would send the bottle back towards her. Mather describes this as "the marine equivalent of bouncing a ball." She has also seen octopuses engaged in what looks like playing with bubbles.

Play is the equivalent of school in the animal kingdom. For many species, play serves as practice for hunting skills or as preparation for battles with competitors for mates. For this reason, Mather finds herself outside the thinking of many of her colleagues, who wonder what adaptive purpose play would serve in a short-lived, solitary animal.

John Forsythe is one of those not ready to agree that the activities cited by Jennifer Mather amount to play. "These are plastic and highly adaptable animals; they are sensory-oriented and very inquisitive about things and deft at handling them, but I still don't see why repetitive procedures should be called play," he notes. If scientists still differ on the question of whether there is incontrovertible evidence that chimps, gorillas, and orangutans display various higher mental abilities, there is no reason they should agree about the abilities of a lowbrow like an octopus.

Okay then, let's not call it play, but what is it? Why would an octopus take an empty pill container and send it toward a water jet and then repeat the actions once the water jet had returned the object? There are alternative explanations, of course: Maybe the octopus was trying to get rid of the bottle and forgot about the container until it came back into its reach. Maybe it was just curious about the jet.

So let's accept this, and accept also that the octopus's navigation of Forsythe's vertical maze might be accomplished through the diligent application of simple strategies. There still remain teasing suggestions of awareness, both in Fiorito's study, flawed though it may be, and in the stories of octopus curiosity and prestidigitation with locks. There are also vaudevillian anecdotes, such as Jean Baul's charge who dramatically showed her contempt for spoiled food. There are sufficient observations to suggest that octopus intelligence may well be more than has thus far been revealed by studies in the lab. Thus it is worth raising the question: Why should an octopus be smart, and how can it be smart without any other of the brain structures we associate with intelligence? Let's consider the why first.

I had suggested earlier that the octopus fails to satisfy all but one of the criteria that various scientists have used to help sort through animals likely to be intelligent. The one characteristic the octopus shares with a number of intelligent animals is the need to seek a wide variety of foods in varied and concealed places. In science speak, such food sources are called "patchy and ephemeral resources." The need to adapt to find hidden foods is one selective pressure that Robert Foley, a biological anthropologist at Cambridge University, attributed to a big jump in brain size in human ancestors two million years ago. That period marks the first time when the ratio of hominid brain size to body weight significantly diverged from the other great apes. The time also marked a period of cooling and drying in Africa.

During such periods, many plants adapt by storing their carbohydrates in tubers and roots underground, making them much harder to find. Foley argues that it is no coincidence that the biggest-brained carnivore (the bear), the biggest-brained ungulate (the pig), and the biggest-brained primate (humans), are all adapted to finding underground and otherwise concealed foods. When foods are patchy and scarce, animals become opportunists, eating tubers one day, but perhaps hunting or scavenging for meat the next.

An animal that has to constantly recalculate the costs and benefits of expending energy while seeking a wide variety of foods needs more brainpower than, say, the leatherback sea turtle that simply roams the seas vacuuming up jellyfish. Catherine Milton did a celebrated study of the relationship of feeding strategy to brain size when she compared spider monkeys and howler monkeys in Latin America. The howler monkeys feast on leaves—nothing more abundant than that in the rain forest—while spider monkeys are fruit eaters and must keep track of fruiting patterns of different rain forest trees as well as the optimal method for moving from food source to food source. While they live side by side, the spider monkey's brain is twice the size of the howler's in comparison to body weight.

If a diet of varied, concealed foods and the need to outwit prey requires a larger brain, there is little wonder that the octopus is smarter than the clam, which sits in the sand, contentedly filtering nutrients with the ebb and flow of the tides. Jennifer Mather and Roland Anderson of the Seattle Aquarium did a study of the feeding strategies of the giant Pacific octopus. The animal seemed to prefer the meat of the Protothaca clam, which has a thick shell and strong adductor muscles, but would more readily consume the easier-to-open mussels and venus clams. They would shatter the thin-shelled mussels and use their tentacles to pull apart the venus clams. To get to the meat of the thick-shelled clams, the octopuses would use their radula, a serrated tooth that they can move back and forth, to drill through the shell, or chip the shell with their beak and then inject a poison that would weaken the adductor muscles.

Then Mather and Anderson got tricky. They wired venus clams shut so the octopuses couldn't use their favored strategy of pulling them apart. No problem—the octopuses would drill or chip the shells. In earlier studies, researchers tried foiling octopuses by coating snails with aluminum or impenetrable dental plastic, and in each case, the octopuses found a way to get at the meal. Mather describes this strategy as doing "whatever it takes to get the job done."

This contrasts markedly with the angler fish, for instance, which cleverly lures prey with an enticing appendage dangling in front of its gaping mouth. As long as small fish are foolish enough to venture near its jaws this strategy will work, but the angler fish would be out of luck if ever forced to alter its food-gathering habits. The flexibility the octopus brings to its food gathering requires more cerebral hardware. Moreover, the ability to adapt its strategy to the situation as it changes could be indicative of a type of awareness. There is, of course, always the danger that what looks like awareness is the result of a simpler strategy—try A to get at the food; if that doesn't work try B, then C, and so on—but Mather notes that the octopus is more targeted in its selection of approaches to a problem than would be the case if it simply ran, dronelike, through a genetically encoded checklist.

A complicated, hard-to-find and hard-to-catch diet might be sufficient to explain the octopus's neurological advantages over its brainless cousins, but other factors may be at work as well. The animal has been designed for extreme dexterity, equipped with a good pair of eyes, and also endowed with an inquisitive nature (the octopus that is always on the lookout for some new opportunity might well be better prepared to live long enough to breed more inquisitive octopuses).

This is what intrigues Hanlon. He suspects that the octopus's large brain is in some way related to the animal's marvelous suite of adaptations that allow it to survive in a marine environment. The animal is equipped for fast, flexible decision-making that enables it to capture fast-moving, competent prey such as crabs and evade swift killers such as barracuda. "John Forsythe and I were in Tahiti watching an octopus move across a coral reef," he recalls. "It traversed four or five different ecosystems and then returned to its den. Its maze-learning abilities were mind-boggling; our divers couldn't do that." He went on to say that when he watches an octopus evade a predator, try to mate, or pursue its own prey, it will rapidly switch between several different strategies, adjusting its behavior on the spot. "The repertoire might be genetically endowed," he says, "but the animal still has to decide which of its array of behaviors to deploy."

In short, Hanlon argues that an octopus needs a big brain because it needs to process a wide variety of sense information and then do a lot of different things. To take but one small piece of its repertoire, he argues that a lot of processing power is needed to control the physical processes that allow the octopus to assume the shape, design, and color of another creature in a fraction of a second.

Despite his deep respect for the animal's incredible behavioral repertoire, Hanlon resists the notion of octopus intelligence simply because the creatures are so vastly different from us. On the other hand, he acknowledges that nature sometimes exploits an ability that arose to serve one purpose but turns out to be useful for others. Timothy Johnston describes these as "ecologically surplus abilities." In the epilogue to their book, *Cephalopod Behaviour*, Hanlon and John Messenger note that this might apply to the octopus and squid's chromatophore system, which, developed as means of concealment, might have stimulated the development of neural structures that permit the animals to use their dazzling color and patterning abilities for signaling as well.

This multi-purpose function might explain why the octopus's optic lobes are relatively large. "What's really strange about the octopus brain is that two-thirds of its central nervous system consists of its optic lobes," he says. He believes that these lobes serve functions beyond the simple processing of information relayed by the animal's eye. "There seems to be some higher order processing, perhaps decision making that derives from visual information, in these lobes," says Hanlon.

With all this decision making going on, isn't it possible there is also some awareness? While a scientist such as Hanlon must ask why, we can ask why not. The motivation to explore its world, combined with an unsurpassed means to do so, may come with side benefits such as a smidgen of awareness.

Scientists do not know what produces intelligence (or even what it is), but if intelligence exists in other animals besides humans, it might be the result of different factors or different combinations of factors in different cases. Dolphins don't necessarily need their big brain for foraging, nor does it seem that they got smart in response to the challenges of returning to the seas some 60 million years ago—Laurie Merino, who has studied the fossil evidence, argues that the big spurt in dolphin brain growth took place many millions of years after they returned to the oceans. But dolphins do have a highly complex social structure, similar in some respects to the social flux of chimpanzees. The correlation between social complexity and intelligence in highly diverse species accounts for the popularity of the hypothesis that the need to understand alliances and complicated hierarchies helped drive the increase in intelligence in *Homo sapiens*.

Examples of orangutan intelligence abound, but what is known about their social structure suggests that it is simpler than the shifting alliances and horse trading that is the glue of chimp society. Some argue that orangs have changed their social groups in response to tens of thousands of years of pressure by humans, while other scientists point to their extraordinarily complex diet, which requires the animal to keep in mind the distribution and fruiting patterns of upwards of one hundred different types of trees. It is safe to say that within the next few decades some compelling new explanation will appear for the evolutionary pressures that seem to make some animals more intelligent than others.

As we place ourselves in judgment of the cognitive abilities of other species, we would also do well to consider the biases we bring to our understanding of intelligence. These biases may be commonsensical, but when dealing with something as nebulous and elusive as intelligence, common sense might be misleading. It is natural to link intelligence to brain size and brain structure, but rather than discount evidence of intelligence from animals with small brains that lack structures associated with intelligence in humans, we should look hard at these anomalies to see whether they are telling us something about intelligence and consciousness. Among the riddles of the octopus is that the structures most associated with high intellectual functions (the vertical lobe system) are larger in simpler, more primitive species than they are in more apparently clever octopus varieties. Similar ambiguities characterize other octopus brain structures associated with memory and learning, leading Hanlon and Messenger to wonder whether we should be looking at brain chemistry rather than brain shape for anatomical indicators of intelligence. Wiring might permit cleverness where brain size suggests it is absent.

Our obsession with brain size may also blind us to what that expensive piece of machinery is doing. Over time, nature routinizes successful behaviors, gradually encoding them genetically, which in some cases frees up mental space for acquiring new behaviors. Octopuses have had the luxury of millions of years to optimize and encode a great deal of behaviors. As a relatively young species, we *Homo sapiens* have not had that opportunity.

There are other subtle ways bias intrudes. Lou Garibaldi notes that we are more inclined to credit intelligence to those animals that interact with the substrate. Thus we are more predisposed to attribute intelligence to the octopus crawling along the bottom, investigating every nook and cranny with its tentacles, than to the cuttlefish that floats in the water column. Scientists who have investigated both species, however, would rank the cuttlefish as a peer of the octopus in terms of brainpower. There are studies underway to try to determine whether the cuttlefish uses its abilities to change its coloration and pattern to send messages to each other.

Finally, let's turn around that dismissive remark that the octopus "has a large brain for an invertebrate." Rather than being an insult, perhaps this remark points to a meaningful measure that we might consider. Perhaps there is some usefulness in looking past sorting devices such as brain size, or even brain-to-body-weight ratio, and instead looking at the relative size of brains between the smallest-brained relative and the largest. Using this as a guide, the octopus is off the scale, since the octopus has come a long way from its nautilus cousins.

The octopus may have come a far longer way in brainpower than we have in relative terms. It's possible to make the argument that intelligence, or at least learning, is relatively more important for the octopus than it is for many other animals. Its vulnerability in a environment replete with big-brained predators, its feeding strategy, visual system, concealment abilities, inquisitive nature and need to learn, its pretzel-man flexibility, its eight tentacles, and God knows what else, all require some measure of incremental brain power. Who knows, maybe the "ecological surplus" of all these abilities are mental capacities far beyond the octopus's place in our great chain of being.

While scientists struggle with these questions, animals will continue to do what they do, oblivious to the debate about the nature and origins of their higher mental abilities. Once one dives into the scientific debate about animal intelligence, it is very easy to lose sight of this simple, yet fundamentally important point. Science cannot decide what is going on in an animal's head, it can only discover what is already there.

The degree to which scientists succeed or fail in coming up with plausible explanations of what an animal is doing when it appears to demonstrate awareness or some other higher mental ability is primarily an issue for science, not an issue for the animals in question (although it has some bearing on animals simply because we tend to be nicer to creatures we deem intelligent—perhaps this explains why we humans tend to be so stingy in acknowledging intelligence in other animals). The octopus that snubbed Jean Baul's spoiled shrimp was either making a statement or it was not. While totally outside the scope of any investigation of octopus intelligence, such anecdotes are important because they remind scientists and others that animals have lives outside our experiments and theorizing. They are also important because they occasionally jolt a scientist into putting aside the blinkered expectations that come with years of exposure to the conventional wisdom on how to look for intelligence, and in which animals.

If we think about octopus snubs, octopus anger, and octopus raids on neighboring tanks, we have to start thinking afresh about the relationship of brain size to intelligence and about different types of intelligence, as well as the forces that make one animal more intelligent than another. That's not a bad thing. The riddle of the octopus may or may not lead to a new approach to animal intelligence, but it is certainly worth pondering.

Chapter Four

THE ORCA THAT FISHED FOR SEAGULLS

Games

Many animals play, most often when they are young. Tigers and other cats practice stalking and hunting skills, gorillas wrestle in preparation for later battles with other males. In captivity, animals play all sorts of games with each other and with their keepers and trainers. Play suggests a lively mind by itself, but sometimes an animal will add a touch that suggests intellectual engagement as well as a sense of fun.

Many animal trainers insist that such engagement is a prerequisite if a trainer is to get results. One of those in this school is Gail Laule, a veteran animal trainer now with Active Environments in California, who has worked for years with a variety of large animals including elephants, gorillas, dolphins, and orcas. Over the years she has worked with a number of orcas at various marine parks.

One featured part of routines is a moment when the ten thousand-pound marine mammals slide up onto a dry surface entirely out of the water before slipping back into the tank. Laule remembers that once she started training the orcas to do this, she would often see them practicing when the trainers were not around. They would try different ways of sliding up onto the surface, as though they were experimenting to find the best way to do the routine. The practice sessions were not prompted by rewards, because there were no people around. At SeaWorld in Orlando, Florida, trainers regularly see orcas practicing aerial gymnastics during free-time periods. Dolphins regularly practice ball-balancing routines as well as flips and spins.

Sometimes the animals introduce their own innovations that then become part of the routine. This was the case with a spectacular stunt in SeaWorld in Orlando, the most visited marine park in the world. During the routine, a trainer will get in front of the orca (when I witnessed the act, the trainer was Liz Thomas, who had been working with orcas since the mid-1980s) and will hold herself still while the killer whale begins pushing on her feet to propel her through the water. With perfect coordination, the big dolphin (orcas are really giant dolphins, not whales) will push her faster and faster until, at terrific speed, she will take a big breath and head on a steep arc towards the bottom of the tank. In one seamless motion the orca will then rocket upwards, leaping straight up into the air with Liz still poised on his nose (or rostrum, to be precise). At the very peak of this jump, perhaps thirty feet in the air, Liz jumps off to the side in a graceful dive while the orca falls back into the water.

It's a spectacular moment, and it grew out of what Chuck Tomkins, the head trainer at SeaWorld, called "playtime," a regular part of the orcas' daily routine. Tomkins says that they can't afford to ever let the animals become bored or anxious, and to avert the daunting prospect of having to deal with idle orcas turned juvenile delinquents, they change the routine and the toys for the animals every day. As one might imagine, the toys are somewhat oversized. Favorites are giant barrels that the orcas will toss back and forth and chase. They also like thick hawsers that they will carry under their pectoral fins and use in games of "keep away" with other orcas. Chuck says that the trainers let the animals choose the toys and games they want to pursue during playtime.

During one such session in the early 1980s, an orca named Ramu invented a game that became the basis of the aerial spectacular. Chuck and Thad Lacinak (another SeaWorld official) were in the pool with Ramu when the orca started pushing on their feet. Then he dove. After a couple of times, Chuck and Thad realized that they could control the direction the orca took. They would subtly shift their body to go down or up, left or right, and the orca would shift to maintain pressure on their feet. With that, they realized that they could train the orcas and integrate this duet into the routine.

"We made a lot of mistakes at first," notes Chuck, "but when we did something the orcas did not like, they would simply tell us 'no.'" Eventually the aerial routine became the dazzling display that wows audiences. Liz says that being propelled by an orca is a little like steering an airplane. "I initiate the jump by heading down. I determine how deep we will go, and I've got to be precise in the direction and speed. Initially, I'd give one, two, or three taps with my foot or hand to let the orca know how fast we should go, but I don't do that much anymore—they already know." She has to be careful with the gas pedal since there is so much horsepower under the hood. The orcas can go so fast that she will tumble off.

Chuck, Liz, and many other trainers insist that the animals enjoy these routines. Chuck argues that every animal in a zoo situation ought to be in training, if only to be mentally stimulated. The evidence, such as impromptu practice sessions, suggests that the animals respond. The trainers will also bring in novel objects for the animals' amusement.

On one occasion, the trainers set up a big mirror on the wet stage upon which the orcas beach themselves during shows. Tomkins says that the orcas were quite curious about the mirror at first, but after a while most ignored it. Not Kotar, however, one of the brightest orcas at SeaWorld, according to Chuck. Kotar first pulled back and glared at this invading orca. Then he touched the mirror. Not satisfied, he went up on one side of the stage to look at it from the side, and then did the same thing from the other side. Still not finding the orca, Chuck says he swam under the stage and looked up. Then Kotar would go back in front of the mirror and do head shakes, only to watch his reflection do head shakes back at him. Long after the other orcas had gone on to other pastimes, Kotar continued to puzzle over the mirror. Notes Chuck, "He sat there and said, 'Don't move that mirror, we're going to figure this thing out.' "

Chuck describes the interaction between the trainers and the orcas as an unwritten conversation. The orcas are active participants in the conversation, and are constantly making sure that the trainers are on their toes. Chuck says that they will test the younger trainers by doing something different than what is asked, and then watch to see how the trainer will react. For instance, a trainer might give the signal (a finger moving in a circle) for an orca to perform the hula. Instead of wagging back and forth, they will raise a pectoral fin. Then they will come to the surface and look at the trainer to see what kind of reaction their response elicited.

Some of these stunts suggest humor. For instance, occasionally the orcas will tease new trainers by repeatedly spitting out salmon they are given as rewards. They don't play this game with older trainers. Instead, if they don't want the salmon, they will simply put it back in the bucket.

The orcas are constantly inventing their own games. The babies will hang around the edge of the tank to lure people to come closer. Once a large enough group is in range, they will drench them with a flick of their tail flukes. They seem to enjoy watching the people scream and yell in reaction. If Chuck approaches the tank wearing a suit and tie, they immediately try to splash him. "They just want to see me react," says Tomkins, "and I can't help it; if I'm drenched wearing a suit, I react."

Their most extraordinary game, however, has nothing to do with humans. In the fall, after the tourists have disappeared from Florida's beaches, the seagulls who feast on leftovers begin scouting for new meal tickets. Every now and then they fly over SeaWorld, and, looking down, see this very inviting blue body of salt water ringed by fast food restaurants and populated by tourists. It must look like gull heaven to a young bird worried about lean pickings during the coming winter.

The orcas have turned this annual migration into their own bird-hunting season. Instead of eating a piece of fish given them by the trainers, they will keep the morsel. Then they will settle quietly under the water and expel the fish toward the surface. As soon as some unsuspecting gull comes down for the fish and alights on the surface, the orca will rise up from the depths and grab the bird.

Most of the time the game is catch and release. Orcas will pull the bird down and then release it, leaving it to fly squawking away to tell its children the avian version of Jonah and the whale. Every now and then, though, notes Chuck, the orcas decide to turn the game into snack time.

There are no stories about orcas using bait in the wild, but then again we don't really know a lot about the feeding behavior of this wide-ranging underwater creature. We do know they use some very inventive strategies such as riding waves to grab seals, and there is some evidence that in the wild mother orcas may teach their babies to strand themselves to grab seals off beaches. One orca in Patagonia was observed grabbing a seal off the beach, letting her baby play with it, and then returning the seal to the shore. (According to whale expert Hal Whitehead, sperm whales also may teach their young to grab seals from beaches, sometimes showing their young how to strand themselves and then return to the water when no seals are around.)

At SeaWorld, Tomkins says that it looks as though the older orcas teach the juveniles how to fish for seagulls. During seagull hunting season, the trainers will see juveniles watch adults and then go off searching the tank for pieces of fish. Orcas are not the only animals to amuse themselves by fishing. Years ago at the Dallas Zoo, the chimps would sometimes take monkey biscuits they are given as treats, and drop them in a small pond near the shore to try to lure the swans within their grasp.

Many other species will invent games, often with other animals. Patricia Simonet, an experimental psychologist at the University of Nevada in Reno, notes that she knew an African gray parrot that hated corn. It would sweep the corn kernels out of its cage. Instead of this being the end of the matter, however, it was the beginning of a game. The parrot would then call the cat, saying "Valentine" in a nice voice. The cat would come over and play soccer with the kernels.

More common than this nice story of interspecific play are stories of interspecific mischief. Jack Bradbury, a distinguished ornithologist at Cornell University, noted that his parrot learned to use the click sound that he used to call the dog. When the dog approached the parrot, the parrot bit the dog on the nose.

Then there is the age-old competition of cats and dogs, who often have to make the best of being in the same household [Note: I've taken pains to limit the number of stories about cats and dogs to prevent the book from being overwhelmed with an endless number of enchanting but unverifiable stories.] In early 2000, I gave a talk at Millersville University in Pennsylvania. After the talk, Dr. Peter Caputo, the university president, told me about the strategy his cat developed to deal with the hassle of being perpetually chased by the family dog. When pursued by the dog, the cat would build a decent lead and then run in a circle a few times, creating a scent trail. Then the cat would step off to the side and watch the dog run around in circles.

At the other end of the size scale, Ivan, a reticulated giraffe at the San Diego Zoo's Wild Animal Park, loves to tease and harass the other animals, according to keepers. It will put two feet on top of the cape buffalo's head, and also make life miserable for some of the other animals, such as the zebra. Once it pushed one of the elands too far, and the big grazer knocked Ivan over, probably to the unvoiced cheers of the other long-suffering ungulates.

Interspecific play happens in the wild as well. In the early summer of 2000, I was up in Churchill, Manitoba, while researching a story on the rapidly changing climate in the Arctic. I'd gone to Churchill because the region on Hudson Bay marks the southern limit of polar bears in North America. As the Arctic has warmed, the sea-ice season has gotten shorter, with ice forming later and melting earlier. This spells trouble for the polar bears, since they do their entire feeding for the year during the sea-ice season, and then sleep through the summer months.

Churchill has given itself the title of "Polar Bear Capital of the World." The town has a good case, because the animals' migratory path often takes the one-thousand-pound predators up through town as they walk north waiting for the ice to firm up. This brings about numerous encounters between wild animals and civilization, for which nature has not really prepared either side. Because the bears get distracted by the pickings in the town dump, for instance, Churchill built a polar bear jail as part of a program to discourage the bears from interrupting their trip to the ice. If a bear begins hanging around town, it will likely feel a prick from the local wildlife enforcer's tranquilizer gun, and then wake up in the jail where it is kept for a day or two before being dropped off some miles north of town. The bears seem to get the message and the recidivism rate is low.

With all these encounters between bears and people, I shouldn't have been surprised when I noticed a photograph of a gigantic polar bear touching noses with a sled dog on the walls of a Churchill diner. My first reaction was that this was some outrageous nature fake, staged to create a photograph that could be sold to tourists. But I was wrong.

Later that day, while talking with Mike Macri, a local guide and photographer, I noticed that he had similar pictures of encounters between the sled dog and the polar bear. This was not some cruel setup—the dog's body language was playful, not terrified as it would have had every right to be, since the polar bear is one of the most formidable predators on the planet. So I asked Mike what was going on.

It turned out that the dog was an Eskimo dog named Bishop. The breed was originally created by crossing explorer dogs with wolves. Somehow Bishop befriended this particular female polar bear as the bears came through town during a recent migration (as the Arctic warms, the bears come through town more often, since the later the ice forms, the further north they walk before heading out onto Hudson Bay). However they met, the bear was in the area for a few days, and when she passed near Bishop, he would call her over to play. The bear was never rough with Bishop, and indeed, seemed to protect the dog. If other bears started approaching, the bear would warn them off. Asked the obvious question—why?—Mike could only speculate. Bears need sparring partners; or maybe the female just responded to the dog, who, being on a long leash tied to a stake, would have been completely vulnerable had the bear decided to make a meal of the encounter.

Canada seems to be the scene of many strange interspecific friendships. West and south of Churchill at Polar Park in Edmonton, an eight-hundred-pound Siberian tiger named Bronson struck up a friendship with a puppy named Lily while Bronson was still a cub. Lily and Bronson were raised together. According to Jay Pratt, a tiger keeper now at the Dallas Zoo, Lily was terrified of everything, but was fearless around Bronson. The dog would occasionally take food away from the tiger. The two were inseparable pals, and would curl up together when it was time to sleep.

Dana Wooster, who cares for the big cats at the Woodland Park Zoo in Seattle, encountered perhaps the strangest bedfellows of all. One of the zoo's lions was getting on in years and seemingly losing interest in life. To try and rekindle his zest for living, the keepers put a live chicken in his cage. This did the trick, but not in the way the keepers had imagined. When they returned to the cage the next morning they found the chicken and lion sleeping peacefully together, with the chicken curled up on the lion's huge forepaw.

At the Columbus Zoo, the elephants have a regularly scheduled period of free time where they can play with the keepers if they like, or use the time for themselves. It's their choice. Harry Peachey notes that Koko, a charismatic and mischievous male Asian elephant, developed a game of fetch that he liked to play with Harry. He would get an empty eight-gallon beer keg and bring it over to Harry next to a pond. Harry would then throw the keg into the water and the ten-thousand-pound, would-be golden retriever would go bounding after it.

After he grabbed the keg with his trunk, Koko would then sink it, filling the keg with water. Then he would wrap his trunk around it and bring it back to Harry so that the keeper could throw it again. What is effortless for an elephant, however, sometimes poses challenges for a keeper. Not many people can throw a sixty-pound, water-filled keg very far, and Harry would then empty it before throwing it again. Koko quickly figured out what Harry was doing, and started emptying the keg before returning it for another throw.

How do we read this elephantine gesture? Perhaps the elephant blindly mimicked Harry's motions, emptying the keg without any idea that this made life easier for the trainer. But elephants are aware of their enormous advantage in strength over humans, as has been evident in countless interactions between the two species. More likely, at least in my mind, is that Koko was showing a touching consideration for us feeble humans.

Finally, I have to recount the most hilarious example of animals adapting to human games I've yet come across, although the story is also one of the most difficult to interpret. The story was passed on to me by e-mail, and I cannot vouch for its authenticity. As the story goes, researchers from Woods Hole Oceanographic Institution stationed in the Antarctic would sometimes organize games of football on one of the ice air strips near the base. Penguins are intensely curious, and the researchers were amused to discover that their games attracted a crowd of penguins who followed the action intently.

One day the scientists arrived to discover that the penguins were already on the field. The birds would line up in two rough groups, and then, according to Doug White, who first posted this story, they would "start squawking and running around, bumping into each other. After a bit of this, they would pick themselves up, and start the process all over again." According to White, they didn't use a ball, but who knows what would have happened had the researchers left one behind. Penguins aren't configured to throw or catch a football, but I'm sure they have the physical skills for soccer.

Appealing as this story is, I'm at a loss to say what it means. It does suggest that the birds can act on observations, and, even more intriguing, somehow act in concert. Left hanging, however, is the question, why? Maybe we shouldn't ask.

Chapter Five

WHERE THE WILD THINGS ARE

Intelligence, Captivity, and Rehabilitation

Many of the stories in this book come from zookeepers, trainers, and other people who deal with animals in zoos, aquariums, marine and theme parks—in other words, in captive situations. It is easier to see intelligence in the interaction of animals and people in captive situations. In part this is because there is a human observing the behavior, and in part because captivity is an unnatural situation that offers an opportunity to see whether and how animals contend with novel circumstances.

Because the animals are not captive by choice, questions of intelligence inevitably become commingled with questions of ethics. The more intelligent the animal, the more likely they are to do something intelligent in captivity, but such examples only beg the question of whether it is right to deprive an intelligent animal of its freedom. On the other hand, the more intelligent an animal, the more difficult it is to return it to the wild, if only because a larger portion of its survival skills will be learned rather than innate.

Most curators, keepers, and trainers are ardent animal lovers, and they prove their dedication every day. On the other hand, the institutions that employ the trainers are often attacked on a variety of grounds, ranging from how the animals are treated and housed to the moral questions of keeping animals in captivity. Because the issue of captivity hangs over much of this book, I feel I should offer my own thoughts on the ethical question of keeping wild animals, and also explore how captivity relates to the study of intelligence, particularly since I have been wrestling with the question for roughly thirty years.

There are few bright lines in any of these questions relating to animals in captivity, but there are some. One of my earlier books, *Silent Partners*, dealt with the fate of the various apes used in language experiments. I found the lives of the animals offered a passion play in which humanity's ambivalent attitude toward the animal kingdom directly affected the fate of the animals. At various points in their lives, animals, treated as personalities and even celebrities during the language experiments, suddenly found themselves transformed into commodities.

For instance, a number of chimps who early in their lives found themselves somewhat pampered as subjects of sign language experiments, ended up in a medical laboratory where they were purposely infected with the AIDS virus as part of a study of potential vaccines. For me, this was a bright line we should not have crossed. At the time the chimps were injected with the virus, no one knew whether the animals would get sick.

I'm fond of Milan Kundera's remark that the true mark of a civilization is how it treats its most helpless members. In infecting a demonstrably sentient and captive animal with what we supposed was a horrible and invariably fatal disease, we failed this test. It was only a matter of luck that it turned out that AIDS does not afflict chimps the way it afflicts humans.

Values always come with a price. It is easy to advocate animal welfare when the animal has no obvious utility as a human surrogate. It is a lot harder to hew to that value when a society is panicked about the potential calamity of a mysterious new disease and there are hundreds of "surplus" chimps that might be used as surrogates because of their close genetic affinity with mankind. It is during such moments, however, that those values become important. The price of protecting chimps from the unknown risks of use in AIDS vaccine protocols is that it might (there are arguments on both sides of this issue) have made it more difficult to test a vaccine for use on humans, but in putting aside notions of respect for other sentient creatures, we pay a price as well by eroding the standards that we avow we will uphold.

Apart from the question of karmic kickback, the use of these animals in AIDS protocols was yet another expression of our utilitarian attitude toward our fellow creatures and the natural world. This attitude clearly is not working. The view of nature that sees animals only as they serve short-term human interests is necessarily blind to the role various creatures play in the maintenance of the planet's life-support systems. One theory of the origin of AIDS holds that the disease was endemic to African primates (the primate version of AIDS, called SIV, has been found in 26 different primate species) and first jumped to humans as they ate or were bitten by primates. Native hunting of apes and monkeys for "bushmeat" is one of the biggest threats to primate populations in Africa, and so long as this practice continues, new strains of AIDS as well as other diseases such as Ebola are likely to jump to humans. In other words, we are inflicting suffering on a close relative because of a disease that we may have contracted by eating that close relative.

Even in the sad AIDS chapter of our treatment of our closest relatives, however, there are shining moments. James Mahoney, the veterinarian in charge of animal welfare at the Laboratory for Experimental Medicine and Surgery in Primates (LEMSIP), the facility where the AIDS vaccines were tested, devoted himself entirely to the welfare of the chimp colony.

After years of searching he found a retirement home for chimps that had been used in these and other medical protocols. The National Sanctuary for Retired Research Primates in New Iberia, Texas, ultimately took sixteen LEMSIP chimps.

The moral issues raised by zoos and marine parks are very different and more complex. Zoos present themselves as defenders of wildlife, preservers of endangered species, and educators of the public. There is an element of truth in all of this, although zoos tend to oversell their role in preserving endangered species. As David Hancocks, the director of Victoria, Australia's Open Range Zoo, and the author of *A Different Nature: the Paradoxical World of Zoos and their Uncertain Future*, points out, the average American zoo maintains fifty-three of the known mammalian species, a ratio of one to thirty-one, and things get worse from there with collections holding about one- to two-thousandths of the known amphibians. The great biologist E. O. Wilson and others have pointed out that bugs, microbes and other invertebrates account for the great mass of life on earth and play a vital role in the functioning of the planet, but they are scarcely acknowledged in zoo collections.

The only real preservation of a species is in the wild. In this regard, zoos such as the Bronx Zoo, the San Diego Zoo, the London Zoo, and many others deserve credit for programs that breed endangered species during times of extreme poaching or warfare, and then reintroduce them into the wild when measures have been taken to protect their native habitat.

William Conway, the former director of the Wildlife Conservation Society, which runs New York City's zoos (including the famed Bronx Zoo) as well as the New York Aquarium, notes that several hundred species have been reintroduced over the years, ranging from tiger beetles in the U.S., to frogs, toads, and birds to large animals such as the Arabian oryx.

The rocky road of the Arabian oryx illustrates the difficulty of putting animals back into the wild. The 250 pound antelope, native to the gravelly deserts of Arabia, went extinct in the wild in 1972. The species was the victim of hunting, after four-wheel-drive vehicles came to the Arabian peninsula and enabled the heedless slaughter of wildlife. Starting with a few animals, a herd gradually grew in the safety of Arizona. After protected areas were established in Oman, Yemen, and Saudi Arabia, a number of reintroductions took place beginning in 1982. The road to recovery has not been easy. According to Conway, the herd in Yemen grew to a population of four hundred before a tribal conflict unleashed a wave of poaching that quickly killed three hundred animals. The remainder have been taken back into captivity.

Conway does not push reintroductions as a rationale for zoos. Apart from the difficulties of maintaining genetic diversity with small populations, the very concept is an admission of defeat about preserving animals in the wild. He does, however, speak eloquently about other roles of zoos in conservation. Worldwide, an estimated 800 million people visit zoos each year, and Conway feels that zoos could use this access to the public to become the major force for conservation in the world in this century.

I hope that he is right. In less enlightened days, zoos all too often were a perverse force for conservation because of the appalling conditions in which they kept animals, creating environmentalism out of pity rather than inspiration. Thankfully, that era is mostly behind us, at least in Europe and the United States.

The Bronx Zoo, for instance, spent lavishly to build a Congo gorilla exhibit, which includes a naturalistic habitat for the zoo's gorilla colony, as well as a series of interactive and educational exhibits that acquaint visitors with the Congo rain forest and the threats faced by that great forest. Conway argues that the exhibit creates a constituency for the rain forest as well as money for conservation. I agree. About 1.5 million visitors a year pass through this exhibit, paying an extra fee of three dollars for the privilege. At the end of their visit they get to determine where their fee will be spent. At the moment they get to choose between spending to protect gorillas, mandrills, okapi, or elephants. Perhaps not surprisingly, the largest percentage have chosen to spend the fees on the gorilla. As of October 2001, the exhibit had raised about $3.3 million for the protection of the animals in the twenty-eight months it had been open.

Some critics argued that the $40 million plus poured into the exhibit might have been better spent in the Congo itself. This is naive. The donors who ponied up for the exhibit (including New York City), were motivated in some significant measure by their desire to contribute to a highly visible project in New York. It is not as though there was a pool of $40 million that could go either to the Bronx Zoo or the Congo.

As for the animals, this is about as good as it is going to get for captive-born gorillas. (I completely agree that, except in cases where inaction will lead to certain death, it is no longer defensible to take gorillas from the wild). All but two of the zoo's gorillas are captive born, and for such animals, an exhibit that offers privacy, reasonable space, opportunities for exercise, social interaction, and intellectual engagement partially mitigates the loss of freedom.

For most of the gorillas in captivity, as for most chimps, orcas, dolphins, and many other animals, return to the wild is a practical impossibility. Certainly there are some highly successful rehabilitation programs, and we will get to those in a moment, but the best candidates for reintroduction are young animals, born in the wild, whose tenure in captivity is relatively short. This excludes the great majority of primates and marine mammals in the United States.

I count myself among those who fervently believe in reintroduction. Every time I see a snow leopard in a zoo, I fantasize about spiriting the animal to the Canadian Rockies, where I would teach it to hunt elk and deer. Over the years, however, I have reported on attempts to reintroduce chimps, dolphins, orangutans, and gorillas to the wild, and have seen just how difficult an undertaking it is to take a chimp version of Private Benjamin and turn her into a Robinson Crusoe.

Prior to writing *Silent Partners*, I traveled to Gambia in West Africa to check up on one of the chimps that had been part of the sign language studies in Norman, Oklahoma, directed by Roger Fouts. Lucy had been raised by two psychologists, Maurice and Jane Temerlin, in their home. When the experiment ended and Lucy matured, the Temerlins sought to find a way to return Lucy to the wild. Janis Carter, one of the graduate students who had worked with Lucy earlier, brought the chimp to Africa and was Lucy's constant companion and teacher in the effort to get this chimpanzee American princess to learn the ways of the wild. I mention this here only because despite extraordinary commitment and sacrifice on the part of Janis Carter, poor Lucy never did achieve full independence before she died. In an oblique way, the difficulties of teaching Lucy about climbing, nest building, and the ins and outs of food gathering—what to eat, how to catch it, and the most efficient way to eat it—all point to the degree of learning that characterizes a chimp's life in the wild.

While it might at first appear that the smarter the animal, the easier it should be to reintroduce it to the wild, the opposite tends to be true. Chimps, gorillas, and orangutans have long periods of immaturity—more than a decade—before they are ready to mate. The long childhoods are necessary because the animals have to acquire the mental as well as physical skills for life in a complex environment replete with dangers. No matter how skilled the human trainer, these skills cannot be acquired in a few weeks. Moreover, even when an animal learns food-gathering skills, it might not survive if it does not have the social and competitive skills to join its wild brethren.

This is particularly true of male chimps and orangutans, who usually aren't equipped to compete and negotiate with other males for several years after sexual maturity. Because a male ape's life is characterized by threats, bluster, and outright fights as they vie for females, they don't typically welcome new potential competitors with open arms. For this reason, wildlife biologists tend to argue that females, particularly young females, are better prospects for reintroduction, since they are more likely to be accepted into an existing wild group.

There have been successful reintroductions, most notably with gorillas in Africa and orangutans in Borneo. One predictor of success has been prior experience in the wild. If the animal is young and wild-born, there is a good chance it can be reminded of what it learned before captivity when it learned specific skills and activated innate abilities. The young can also acquire new skills from other animals. After more than eight years in captivity, however, the chances for success drop dramatically.

The success of efforts to reintroduce orangutans is remarkable considering the complexities of their life and the array of threats they face. Orangutans live in one of the world's most complicated systems, the ancient rain forests of Borneo and Sumatra. Considered to be the oldest tropical forests on earth, the lowland forests of Borneo contain an astonishing variety of creatures, ranging from flying squirrels and snakes to pygmy rhinos and sun bears. During one trip through the forest I came upon what looked like the stinking remains of a rotting carcass. In fact, it was a blooming Rafflesia, the world's largest flower (it sometimes weighs more than one hundred pounds), which mimics offal in order to attract flies, which serve as the flower's pollinators. One hectare of Borneo rain forest might contain five hundred different species of tree, and it behooves a big, fruit-eating animal like the orangutan to know the fruiting patterns of a bewildering variety of flora. Orangs eat up to four hundred different foods, a far more complex diet than that of the fruit-eating spider monkey.

The red ape also has to contend with more predators than Latin American primates do. While there are jaguars and ocelots in Latin America, the Sumatran orangutan is hunted by tigers (which might explain why this subspecies spends more time in trees than its Borneo-based cousins). And while humans threaten all primates around the world, our presence in Latin America extends back between ten thousand and twenty thousand years, while humans have been hunting orangs in Borneo for forty thousand years and perhaps longer.

If man has long been a factor in orangutan life (some argue that hunting by humans explains the animal's solitary habits), this has never been more true than today. Orangs are hunted by poachers, crowded out by farmers and loggers, burned out by fires set by both groups, and otherwise starved by the transformation of the land. The destruction of Indonesia's forests is the greatest ecological tragedy of the current era.

For all its diversity, almost all of the trees that make up the rain forest canopy in Borneo and Sumatra are dipterocarps, a class of flora that has a unique strategy for reproduction called "masting." This simply means that to foil predators, the trees suddenly produce overwhelming amounts of fruit at unpredictable intervals. Worked out by nature, the basis of the strategy is to produce so many seeds that even with thousands of seed-eating creatures around there will be enough left over for the forest to regenerate.

Nature did not bargain on mankind however, and work by biologist Lisa Curran of Yale University has demonstrated that the combination of tree cutting and the increased presence of humans has upset the implicit calculations behind masting. With fewer trees and more humans, all the fruit produced tends to end up in something's stomach. Thus, as forests shrink, they are not regenerating, even when people leave after logging. This has dire short-term implications for the wondrous animals of Borneo, including orangutans. The bleak scenario threatens humans as well, since the forest stores water, holds soils, and stabilizes climate. In other parts of the world, the cutting of forests has sometimes been followed by the gradual loss of rainfall and the hardening of soils until what was once lush, green, and productive becomes desiccated and lifeless.

I have made several trips to Indonesia. Over the years I've traveled to Borneo and Sumatra to report on orangutans, to research an article on the loss of indigenous knowledge around the world as tribes abandon their ways, and to see firsthand what has become ground zero in the ongoing destruction of the world's rain forests. The first time I flew over Borneo in 1971, the great island was almost entirely forested. Since then great swaths of the island's forests have been cut, burned, or otherwise degraded. The Borneo rain forest is perhaps the richest and oldest wet tropical forest on earth, and its pell-mell destruction has only accelerated despite regular reports from the front.

Fourteen million hectares of Indonesian forest burned during two intense El Niños (a regular global shift in weather patterns that often is accompanied by drought in Indonesia), when logging interests and farmers took advantage of dry conditions to set fires to clear land. Loggers, abetted by a complaisant ministry of forests, have cleared much of the Malaysian states of Sarawak and Sabah. In Indonesian Borneo, forests fall to legal and illegal logging operations, as well as to forest clearing by migrants from other islands.

The most visible victims of this destruction are orangutans, particularly the thousands of young orangutans who are orphaned by fire, logging, or hunting. Typically, the mother dies protecting her infant as a tree is felled. If there is any good news in this tragedy, it is that a number of dedicated European, American, and Indonesian scientists have been making heroic efforts to save these orphans and return them to the wild. One of these sites is the Balikpapan Orangutan Survival Foundation, founded in 1991 by Willie Smits, a Dutch tropical ecologist. BOSF runs the Wanarisit station about forty kilometers outside of Balikpapan in eastern Kaminantan.

Wanarisit is the largest such facility in the world, with a capacity of about two hundred orangutans at any given time. As of this writing, Wanarisit is filled to capacity as out-of-control logging, coupled with a welcome increase in attention to the plight of orangutans, has created a flood of orphans. On November 3 and 4 of 2001, Wanarisit released forty-five orangutans back into the one-hundred-thousand-hectare Meratus forest, the largest release ever (the timing was driven by the fruiting season).

These orangutans were successful graduates of a well-thought-through rehabilitation program, in which orangutans are gradually reacquainted by humans and other orangs with the intricacies of climbing and finding food in the wild. After a quarantine during which it is checked for TB, hepatitis, malaria, and other diseases the animal might have picked up from humans, the young orang will begin its reeducation by being introduced to other orangs of similar age, either in a baby nursery or a halfway house where the orphans can learn to climb trees and find fruit in the trees in a fenced-in area. Much of this they acquire by observing other orangutans who either had more experience in the wild or more time at the center.

Typically, an animal might spend three to four months in the halfway house before it is judged ready for reintroduction. Being ready means that they are healthy and eating well, have good climbing skills, get along with playmates, and are independent. At this point, they are tranquilized, put in cages and driven five hours to the forest. Once there, the cages are carried 1.5 kilometers into the forest to the release site, where the apes are put in a big cage with an opening on the top. The orangutans are then fed and left overnight.

The big moment comes the next morning when the top of the cage is opened and the animals are freed to climb up into the trees above. Almost all the animals take right to the trees. Those reluctant to leave are given some fruit, but usually they, too, will join their compatriots they see climbing around them.

Every now and then an orangutan will get injured and come back. Willie remembers one orangutan that was released at five years old and returned later with a wound on his leg. The wild orang allowed Dr. Joe Cuthberson to sew up the wound using only a local anesthetic. Once fixed up, the orangutan proudly showed his stitches to another orang.

Ann Russon, an associate professor at York University in Toronto who has spent several years at Wanarisit, remembers one attractive adolescent female named Maya who got hurt when caught up in a melee involving two males fighting for her attention. She limped back to the camp with a broken arm and a hurt leg. Ordinarily an orang would be wary of a human touching it, but when hurt it seems to know that humans can help, says Russon, and the young female was quite placid when fitted with a plastic cast and brought into the caged area to recuperate. At one point, Ann was walking by her cage and said, "Maya, aren't you going to show me your arm?" Maya came up to the bars, says Ann, and with the most pitiful "poor me" expression on her face, pressed the cast against the bars and pointed to the place where the arm was broken.

The Wanarisit program gives me a lot of hope. If it is possible to successfully return a highly intelligent animal to the forests in an ecological war zone such as Borneo, it should be possible to return a host of other animals to less troubled areas. Indeed, in Africa there is a similar success story.

The gorilla program in the Congo was set up and funded by the late John Aspinall, a true British eccentric and passionate animal lover (who had it in his will that no harm should come to any of his tigers if he was killed by one of them while in their cage at Howlett's, the private zoo he founded near Canterbury, England). I met Aspinall during my reporting of a long story exploring the mingled destinies and natures of apes and humans, entitled "Apes and Humans," that was published by *National Geographic* in 1992. Aspinall made his fortune through his ownership of casinos in London, and as a gambler he was willing to assume risks that no institution would dare take.

Despite owning a zoo, which he saw as a safe house for creatures hunted and crowded out by humanity in the wild, Aspinall believed an animal's place was in the wild. He was also very partial to gorillas, once explaining, "Being English, I admire people who are not too emotional, and gorillas have dignity, equanimity and aloofness." Putting his money where his mouth was, Aspinall first built a wonderful facility in Brazzaville to house orphans and other confiscated gorillas while they were reeducated for the wild.

This was only a staging area, however, while his staff looked for a protected expanse of forest where the animals might be reintroduced without competing with existing populations. They found just such a spot in the Lefini Wildlife Reserve, where a 45,000-hectare expanse of gallery forest offered the refuge he was looking for. Aspinall's audaciousness centered around his willingness to risk failure in his efforts to get the animals back into the forest.

He once told me that early attempts might fail, but that those ape pioneers might pave the way for a much better life for other captive gorillas that, as of then, had no possibility to return to the wild. This is certainly not a risk that any zoo would be prepared to take, and I felt a little ambivalent about it because it was not his life he was talking about, but the lives of captive animals who had no say in the matter. On the other hand, it was absolutely essential that some program be established. Under pressure from conservationists, African wildlife officials were seizing gorillas from traffickers and hunters and, before John Aspinall came along, no one had any idea what to do with them.

In 1996, the first group of adolescents was released in Lefini. One animal died, but the others adapted successfully. Since then the program has worked so well that most captured orphans are taken directly to a staging area in the forest. As is the case with the successful release of orangutans, however, the key to this program is that the animals are young and have fresh memories of the wild. If there is a limitation in this program, it is that the 45,000-hectare area of protected forest can only absorb so many gorillas. As gorillas leave the protected area they become fair game for native hunters, who kill the animals for sale as meat in Brazzaville.

The constraints that limit the prospects for rehabilitation apply under the water as well. Many purists balk at the supposed indignity of using a magnificent animal like an orca for entertainment. Certainly, I agree that orcas should not be taken from the wild for use in such shows. The issue of what to do with captive-born orcas, and those that have spent most of their lives in captivity, is more complicated.

As is the case with chimps, part of the difficulty in returning orcas to the wild derives from their intelligence and complex social structure. The animals acquire an enormous amount of hunting and survival skills from their mothers and other adults. In the wild, orcas have been observed in what looked like attempts to teach young members of the group how to make the bubble rings orcas create to make a "net" around fish. As noted, mother orcas in Patagonia have been observed showing their young how to strand and free themselves with incoming and outgoing waves as a hunting technique for grabbing seals from the beach. An orca has to learn an enormous amount about what is good to eat and what is not, which prey are not worth the effort, the migratory patterns of various fish and marine mammals, and local knowledge about their home area. Some of this they pick up by observation, some might be the result of active teaching, but only a portion of it is innate. It is hard enough for a human to teach a chimp how to build a nest high up in a tree or choose among different fruits and tubers, but working with a marine mammal entails an entirely new set of problems for landlubbers.

Then there is the problem of monitoring the animal once it is released. In Borneo, if an orangutan gets in trouble it will often try to get back to the sanctuary where it was rehabilitated, and field assistants can keep loose tabs on the animals in the wild. With wide-ranging marine mammals, that chore is vastly more complicated and expensive. The very first article I wrote for *Time* concerned the release of two dolphins, Joe and Rosie, who had been used in the making of the film, *The Day of the Dolphin*. Fitted with transmitters and given extensive training, the two dolphins were released in the rich tidal waters off South Carolina. Efforts to monitor them proved very short-lived, however, because the transmitters either stopped working or fell off.

The most celebrated attempt to return an orca to the wild involved another marine mammal who gained celebrity as the star of a film. This was Keiko, who played Willy in the movie *Free Willy*. Keiko had been captured by Icelandic fisherman as a juvenile in 1979 and then spent much of his life in an inadequate facility in Mexico City's Chapultepec Park before he got his shot in Hollywood. Through the generosity of private donors like Craig McCaw and Jerry and Ani Moss, and money contributed by Warner Bros., Keiko was first transferred to a two-million-gallon tank at the Oregon Coast Aquarium, where his health was restored and human instructors tried to teach him to chase and catch live fish. After three years the nine-thousand-pound killer whale was transferred (by UPS!) to a floating pen in the harbor of the Westmann Islands in Iceland, where he has the opportunity, but not the necessity, to reacquaint himself with the waters that had been his birthplace.

As of this writing, Keiko will venture out from his pen into open waters (accompanied by human observers), but he always returns to his gigantic pen. He has not yet demonstrated any inclination to fish. Indeed, no human could teach the kind of acrobatic fishing skills orcas routinely use in the wild, such as herding herring and then tail-slapping a school to stun the fish. Keiko's preferred acrobatic fishing technique is to jump out of the water and take a dead fish from a trainer.

Even if Keiko becomes an accomplished fisherman, other hurdles remain. Orcas are highly territorial, and Keiko would stand a much better chance of joining one of the wild orca social groups in the area if he were a she rather than a he. Now that it is beginning to look like Keiko's tenure in captivity will stretch out indefinitely, and with the stock market collapse crimping the wallets of donors such as Craig McCaw, various critics have begun second-guessing every aspect of this high-profile venture, from the whale's psychological preparation to advance work on locating Keiko's original pod. Still, at least for the moment, with his access to natural surroundings, Keiko enjoys a captivity that would be the envy of most other captive orcas.

The evidence thus far is that with the exception of animals who are being returned to the wild after a relatively brief time in captivity, the return of the smarter animals to the wild will continue to be a rarity. Rather than discouraging those who would help captive animals, recognizing the difficulties of returning animals to the wild should encourage creative thinking. Around the world, people have been buying land and establishing sanctuaries that offer room to roam, if not natural conditions for species ranging from tigers to rhino.

Zoos walk a fine line between attempts to make exhibits natural, accessible to the public, and interesting to the animals. This is no easy task. David Hancocks, a fiery reformer among zoo directors, points out that for all the attention given to "naturalistic exhibits," the real-looking mud wallow the visitor sees is likely made out of plastic and thus of no use whatsoever to a cape buffalo or an elephant. An exhibit may contain trees or other foliage, but if they are protected by hot wires, they become more a source of frustration (and mischief) than an amenity for the animals. Hancocks cites Terry Maple, the director of Zoo Atlanta, who, rather than put trees off limits to the gorilla colony, told the exhibit designer to "get cheaper trees!" Finally, when not in front of the public, many animals spend their time in barred cages little changed since the prison-like conditions of Regents Park Zoo, the first modern zoo opened to the public in London in 1828.

Making things interesting for the animals can lead in some counterintuitive and even seemingly "unnatural" directions. In 1950 the ethologist Heini Hediger, then director of the Basel Zoo in Switzerland, published *Wild Animals in Captivity.* Among other things, he noted that humans would not be able to reproduce the wild in captivity, and so the best thing they might do is make captivity interesting. This does not necessarily mean natural.

Harry Peachey, perhaps the dean of American elephant keepers, notes that at the Columbus Zoo they constructed a new enclosure with gaps between the horizontal bars so that the naturally inquisitive elephants could monitor what was going on outside. He says that elephants will follow keepers around as they work outside, just keeping an eye on things. In one part of the enclosure where there is a solid wall, the keepers installed an eyehole so that they can look inside before entering. The elephants like this innovation and use it themselves to keep tabs on the keepers. Harry says that it can be unnerving the first time someone looks through the hole and sees a giant eye peering back at them. Koko, who is nine-and-a-half-feet tall, has to go to some trouble to lower himself to see through the eye hole, which is six feet off the ground.

Another innovation introduced by the Columbus Zoo is a shower over a pool that the elephants can operate themselves. When first installed, automatic controls turned the shower on or off on a regular schedule, but then, at the suggestion of well-known landscape architect and zoo exhibit designer John Coe, they decided to install a proximity detector that allowed the elephants to turn on the shower themselves. The detector consists of a plate that activates the shower if touched or if an object approaches within a half inch. At first they timed the resulting shower to last fifteen seconds to encourage the animals to learn how to use the detector, but then lengthened the shower period to forty-five seconds. They also installed a counting device to monitor how many times the animals used the shower.

The elephants took to the device like pigs to a wallow. In one twenty-four-hour period, for instance, the counter recorded sixty-five showers. More interesting were the innovative uses the animals figured out for their new toy. One African elephant named Penny would turn it on just to watch the water spill down. Others used the shower as a fountain for drinking water. On their own, they also decided that the shower was a good way to dampen hay, which elephants like to do before eating it.

The shower also revealed interesting social dynamics among the elephants. Belinda, the dominant elephant in one group of three, delighted in using the shower, but would not turn it on herself. When she wanted a shower, she would look over her shoulder at one of the others, who would take the hint and turn on the water for their leader. Perhaps Belinda figured that operating machinery was beneath a figure of her stature, or maybe she couldn't figure the damn gizmo out. In any event, the elephant innovations in the use of the shower offered a vivid glimpse of the ways in which animals can appropriate a piece of technology for their own purposes.

Keeping things interesting for the animals can lead zoo designers in some unusual directions. Some of the happiest tigers in captivity are at Marine World Africa USA in Vallejo, California. The exhibit has a large tank with a glass wall so that viewers can watch from safety. Between two and four times a day trainers will get in the pool with the tigers (the hand-reared Bengal tigers are habituated with the trainers from infancy, relationships reinforced by daily encounters with the animals) and toss chunks of meat into the water, giving the big cats the opportunity to dive for their meal. They seem to love it, while visitors get the very rare treat of being able to watch a tiger swim.

Some people, sensitive to the dignity of animals, disapprove of these and other spectacles, such as having sea lions or dolphins balance objects on their snouts. Lou Garibaldi notes that for the sea lion, at least, such games derive from abilities that serve a serious purpose in the wild. When capturing fish, the sea lion must keep balanced pressure on its prey while it positions itself to take the fish in its mouth. Besides, says Garibaldi, in ball-balancing shows the sea lions often cheat, propping the ball in position with their whiskers to keep it steady.

Captivity need not seem like a prison sentence. On the other hand, statements that animals are better off in captivity because they are ensured of food, safety, and veterinary care are preposterous. The most recent person to make this argument was Ken Feld, the chairman and producer of Ringling Bros. and Barnum & Bailey Circus, whose company was recently acquitted of abusing its elephants in a case brought by animal rights groups. Striking back in a full-page ad published in the *New York Times*, Feld argued that the "wild" really no longer exists and that elephants "are dying out there." He implied strongly that they were better off in captivity.

There is no doubt that Asian elephants face a dire future, but the wild is where the battle for the animals' future will be won or lost. If nature's incentives work for animals as they do for us, their fulfillment comes not from security but from expressing abilities for which they have been equipped by the ancient flux of natural selection. Saying that a tiger is better off in captivity than hunting in Primorskikri is like saying that a Tuarig nomad is better off flipping hamburgers at McDonald's because such jobs get people into the cash economy. If it's true, it is very, very sad.

Zoos serve a vital purpose, but they are not ideal. Their importance has risen in direct proportion to humanity's destruction of wildlife and habitat around the world. Gail Laule, a gifted animal trainer, put it best: "Those of us who deal with animals in captivity should do so with a guilty conscience."

Chapter Six

ORANGUTAN THEFTS AND ELEPHANT DEMOLITION

Tools

Imagine some time in the very distant future. Humanity has gone the way of other species into extinction, and enough time has passed that the planet has restored its natural equilibrium. Perhaps another highly intelligent species has arisen, or perhaps come visiting from another planet. Whichever species turns out to be our intelligent successor, they will likely be interested in the planet's past. Sifting through whatever landscape we leave behind when we pass from the stage (and I hope that we actually do leave a landscape behind), these future paleontologists will probably find fossilized remains of humanity just as we find hominid bones today. But they will find other artifacts of humanity as well. If our bones survive through future ages, so will some remnants of our buildings, dams, roads, and other physical alterations of the earth.

Perhaps, then, we will be remembered in the future as a species that built things. It was not all that long ago that we humans thought we were the only species to make and use tools and gave ourselves the name *Homo faber*—man the craftsman. The notable historical figures who singled out toolmaking as humanity's unique ability included Ben Franklin and British philosopher Thomas Carlyle. Subsequently, naturalists have discovered scores of animals, from bugs to birds, that employ tools. Implements include a wide range of sticks, stones, and leaves. Chimps in the Tai Forest in the Ivory Coast use rocks and tree roots as platforms upon which they rest various nuts, which they smash with rocks and clubs. Crows in New Caledonia use a tool kit of various shaped and sized twigs to extract different insects from foliage.

It is not terribly surprising that chimps and crows might use tools, since both are recognized for their cleverness, but tool use turns out to be surprisingly widespread. At the San Diego Zoo's Wild Animal Park, condor keepers say that the giant birds will follow them around and occasionally try to poke them through the mesh of the cage with sticks or feathers that they hold in their beaks. Even the octopuses that hold clamshells over themselves as they scamper across the muddy ocean bottom off of New England might be described as tool users.

As the number of known tool-using animals has increased, scientists have also done what they always do when some supposedly uniquely human ability turns out to be widely shared: they have raised the bar for what constitutes tool use. Using one tool for one purpose could be genetically encoded, but modifying a tool or selecting various tools for different purposes according to attributes that are relevant to the task at hand may indicate that the animal has some sense of what is needed to accomplish some task.

While I fully expect that there is continuity between animal and human toolmaking abilities, the differences between animal and human tool use are hardly trivial. No other animal even comes close to our ability to alter the environment. But it is also important to note that all the great earth works, buildings, and monuments that we will someday leave behind are extraordinarily recent in evolutionary terms. If some plague had wiped out humanity eight thousand years ago, future paleontologists would scarcely distinguish our material culture from that of other primates.

Yet these *Homo sapiens* ancestors were as smart as we are today. Despite all the brainpower at their disposal they altered the environment very little as ten thousand generations came and went—over ninety percent of the time our species has been on the planet. Why is it that only in the last few thousand years have we left such a profound mark on the planet? Why didn't we earlier?

The answer might be as simple as the weather. As noted earlier, we may owe our existence to periods of rapid cooling and drying in Africa that coincided with rapid evolutionary change in our hominid ancestors. Unstable climate due to re-current ice ages also characterized most of the history of *Homo Sapiens* until the last ice age ended a little over ten thousand years ago. Since then, the climate has had its ups and downs, but the Holocene (as the present period is called) has still been remarkably benign compared to previous eras.

While the old saying holds that "necessity is the mother of invention," the more favorable climate conditions for innova-tion are those fat periods when both individuals and species have a surplus that lowers the risk of failure. In the case of hu-mans, the good weather of the Holocene allowed human num-bers to expand rapidly, and many of the original artifacts of our material culture, including irrigation systems, dams, granaries, roads, and fortifications, had to do with solving the problems of supplying and defending burgeoning human communities. The advent of cities both pooled human ingenuity and re-quired it, but the prerequisite for cities may have been an envi-ronment that produced enough surplus to free humans for specialization and allow the growth of large communities. Had the weather remained lousy a bit longer in geological time, hu-manity might never have clustered in sufficient numbers to allow the runaway growth of material culture.

Since the human brain was equipped to build the space shut-tle long before NASA existed, it is possible that the mental abilities necessary for technology originally developed to serve other purposes. More to the point, if we had vastly greater abilities to make and use tools than was evident for most of our time on earth, maybe some other animals have more ability to use tools than we have seen in the evidence from the wild. Even with the most enriched environment, however, I wouldn't expect to find anything close to even the most primitive human material culture in the animal world. Technology is related to brain size and configuration, and the only animals that remotely compare in terms of encephalization (ratio of brain-to-body weight developed by Harry Jerison as a crude measure of braininess) are the dolphins, which have a large brain like humans, but one very differently organized. Still, if changed circumstances can bring out the genius in humanity, the same might be true for other animals.

Perhaps this explains the mystery of the orangutan, which in the wild shows only glimpses of the engineering abilities that seem to flower in captivity. Fu Manchu used a wire to pick a lock; another orangutan named Jonathan fashioned a probe out of a piece of cardboard which he used to unfasten a security pin that held the doors on his cage closed. Orangutans have made insulating gloves out of straw in order to climb over electrified fences. One orangutan in Borneo is reported to have untied a rowboat, paddled it across a river, and then tied it to a tree on the other side while it explored. Perhaps the most extraordinary story of all, however, involves a series of brazen thefts perpetrated by a female orangutan in Borneo. The mischief involved toolmaking, tool use, and deception, as well as great dexterity. Unyil's feats (for this is the name of the orangutan in question) require a little more background on the species and its present situation in Borneo.

Modern orangutans date back between two and five million years, depending on which scientist is interpreting the fossil record. Today they are confined to the islands of Borneo (which is divided between Malaysia and Indonesia) and Sumatra. In ancient times, orangutans were widely distributed through Southeast Asia, and probably got to the islands either by some now-submerged land bridge, or carried by currents on some floating tree (strange as it sounds, rafting accounts for the dispersal of a wide range of species to different islands and continents). Either through climate change, disease, predation, overcrowding, or some combination of these factors, orangutans disappeared from the continents.

The conventional wisdom is that the orang is among our more distant ape relatives, splitting off from a common ancestor some eight to twelve million years ago. By contrast, analysis of DNA suggests that humans and chimps may have diverged as recently as five million years before the present. DNA analysis also suggests that chimps are closer relatives than orangutans since we share ninety-nine percent of our genes with chimps and about ninety-eight percent with orangutans. There are some lingering questions about the reliability of the "molecular clock" used for dating, since it depends on changes in mitochondrial DNA that could possibly vary. Moreover, it is theoretically possible that humans share more significant genes with orangutans than with chimpanzees, even if the entire genetic code has more overlap with chimpanzees. While it is very unlikely that orangutans are more meaningfully related to humans than chimps, it is not impossible.

There is a reason that various scientists raise this question: Orangutans simply display more humanlike behavior than chimps and gorillas. Chimps and gorillas are distinctly configured to "knuckle-walk," which means that they support part of their weight on their knuckles when they move across the ground. Humans lack that adaptation, but so do orangutans. Some explain this anomaly by arguing that knuckle-walking is a recent development that occurred after chimps, gorillas, and bonobos split from our common ancestor. There are other well-documented similarities, such as the absence of genital swellings that are characteristic of chimps during mating periods, and female sexual receptivity that is not limited to periods of estrus. The similarities between humans and orangutans might bespeak close kinship, or more likely, convergent evolution, the phrase used to describe the process by which nature produces similar adaptations in completely different creatures.

I will have more to say about this powerful concept later, but if selective pressures in their native rain forests seem to have produced humanlike physical adaptations, they also seem to have produced a very humanlike facility with tools. In *The Parrot's Lament* I offered a number of examples of orangutan engineering from zoos. Since then, even more extraordinary stories have surfaced, many of them from the experiences of scientists and staff working at the Wanarisit rehabilitation site. These stories also suggest an answer to the mystery of the origins of these abilities that seem to flower in captivity.

By far the most stunning story to come out of Wanarisit involves an animal that came to the center in 1992. This was a twelve-year-old female they named Unyil. She was the fifty-eighth orangutan to arrive at Wanarisit. The center got the orangutan from an Indonesian colonel, the latest of a series of government officials in Banjarmasin who had owned the animal. As each high official was transferred or moved on, he passed on Unyil to his replacement. According to Willie Smits, the young female had been kept in unspeakable conditions, and her owner only turned in the orangutan because the animal was deathly ill and he did not want her to die in his possession (despite the chaos in Indonesia, wildlife officials are making an effort to better enforce laws protecting orangutans).

Unyil had been kept in quarters so small that she could not

stand up and her arms stuck out from her sides. The colonel had obviously kept the animal as a novelty, since she came to the facility with a smoking habit. She also came with a host of diseases, including a positive test for tuberculosis (because of a high number of false positives in tests of orangutans, however, this did not necessarily mean she had the disease). Willie remembers that when she was released from her cage, the first thing she wanted was a hug.

While the center staff began drug therapy for her many ailments, Unyil was kept in a quarantine facility. The setup consisted of two ranks of cages facing each other across a wide alley, where the staff would pile fruits and other foods out of reach of the animals in the cages. About two weeks after her arrival, Willie noticed that there were mutterings and dissension among the Indonesian staff. Assistants were accusing other assistants of theft. It was a troublesome situation and Willie instructed his chief assistant, a man named Muhibir (who went by the nickname Udin), to find the thief and fire him.

The technician decided to set up clandestine surveillance and found a concealed perch outside the building where he could peek in and observe the morning routine. At first he saw nothing out of the usual. At seven a.m., the station workers brought in the fruits and leaves and put them in the middle of the alley. After feeding the orangutans they closed up at about 9:30 and left. The chief-technician-turned-undercover-operative maintained his vigilance.

After things quieted down, the technician noticed that Unyil had started to move around. She began pulling long red hairs from her shoulder. When she had accumulated several long hairs, she then tied them together into a rope using both lips and fingers (orangutans tend to favor their lips when tying knots—I've watched them do this—because they have more precision in using their lips in fine tasks than they do using their fingers). After she had made a rope of about 60 centimeters, Unyil began looking around the cage. She clearly had something in mind.

Her devious designs became clear a few minutes later when she found a banana peel. She tied the rope around the end of the banana peel. With this weight now securely fixed, she held one end of her rope while she tossed the weight into the pile of fruits. She repeated the process until she snagged an apple, and by jerking the line pulled the fruit within reach of her long arms.

Udin now knew who was stealing the fruit, but he was soon to discover the reason that Unyil had been able to get away with her stealing for so long without being discovered. Unyil would simply eat the entire apple, seeds and all, but when she snagged a mango she was faced with the problem of where to put the large pit. Her solution was to tip the lid of the septic tank and toss the large seed into a place where no one would look for it. Says Willie, with every evidence of pride in his young Fagin, "She not only knew how to commit the crime, but she knew how to conceal the evidence!" After a year in captivity, Unyil was deemed fit to live in the forest and she was released in Sungai Wain.

It was only the assistant who witnessed the incident, and memory tends to embellish, but orangutans have been observed doing every behavior described in this story. I've seen an orangutan tie a knot with its lips and tongue, and keepers at zoos regularly report on the orangutan penchant for weaving and knot tying. Ann Russon notes that in the wild, orangutans have been observed tying two liana vines together when one is not strong enough to bear an animal's weight.

Russon also has an answer to the puzzle of orangutan tool use. The animals are the engineers of the zoo menagerie, but examples of orangutan tool use in the wild have been few and far between compared with the rich and varied material culture of

chimpanzees. Chimps use a wide variety of tools to fish for termites, crack nuts, and get at pith in palm trees. Russon argues
that orangutans also use a great variety of tools in the wild, but
we don't regard it as tool use because of an arbitrary insistence
that an implement must be detached and shaped in order to be
considered a tool. Russon notes that "detachment is a four-
letter word to an orangutan." The orangutan is the most arbo-
real of the large great apes, and spends most of its time high up
in precarious perches where it is betting its life that fragile
branches will remain attached. If we look instead at the animal's purposeful alteration of its physical environment to
achieve various ends, Russon argues, we would see orangutans using and fashioning rungless ladders, lounge chairs,
"down elevators," lifts, and swings, among other things.

Russon has seen orangutans pull two saplings together,
and, holding one in each arm and leaning the tops against
trees, use the saplings as a rungless ladder. Once in the trees,
orangs will take advantage of the suppleness of saplings to
lower themselves slowly to the ground as the trees bend under
their weight. Orangutans construct a lounge chair by taking
two 1.5-meter branches and crossing them in an "X" pattern,
braced so that the ape can lean back and relax. The lift is
slightly more complicated. Orangs will find a perch on one
springy branch and then use one arm to hold on to a higher
branch under tension, and then use the lever to move higher
and lower to get to food.

Russon argues that some of the "tool use" she has observed
indicates that the animals are capable of thinking about their
own actions and then adjusting their thinking to improve on
the results. Dubbed metacognition, the ability to reflect on and
adjust thinking is an indicator of consciousness. She cites as
one example the case of an orangutan she observed who made
several futile attempts to use a sapling to cross a gap to get to a
palm tree (orangutans have a particular fondness for heart of

palm). Each foray would take the orangutan tantalizingly close to his target, but he could not reach across the remaining four or five centimeters. After trying this six times, the orang paused for a moment to survey the sapling he was using. Then he partially broke off a branch he had been using to extend his reach, creating a longer "handle." The extra few inches permitted the orangutan to grab the palm tree and enjoy his salad.

One of the most striking aspects of orangutan behavior in captivity is the animal's ability to focus. Unlike chimps, in whom energy seems to build up explosively, limiting their attention span, orangutans seem to be able to worry about a problem for extended periods of time. Russon has observed them go off on mysterious building projects at Wanarisit, in which they will spend half an hour or more arranging sticks or building a pile. She has no idea what the purpose of these activities is, but they are clearly organized rather than random.

What is it that permits the orangutan to concentrate better than its fellow great apes? One clue may be in the brain. Research by Katerina Semendeferi of the University of California, San Diego, has shown that an area of the brain associated with emotional reactivity is smaller in orangutans than in chimps. Why would an orangutan be less emotionally reactive than a chimp? Chimps have a much more intense social life on a daily basis. The answer may simply be that enhanced emotional reactivity may better prepare chimps for the rough and tumble life in a high-energy group.

Or, the answer may lie in the forest. Russon recalls once watching an adult male orangutan, perched twelve meters up in a palm tree, spend over one hundred minutes without a break taking apart the mature stems of the tree in order to get at the pith. Getting heart of palm from young stems is a relatively straightforward process of stripping the frond. To get at the pith of the mature frond, however, the orangutan has to work past nasty spines, then strip off a leathery covering before getting to a point where the animal can crack open the inner part of the frond to get at the delicacy.

The task requires strength, but it also requires a complicated series of actions that have to be done in a particular order. Russon has noticed that adolescent males tend to lead in this endeavor. In this particular case, the orangutan worked about forty minutes apiece on three different fronds before pausing. The rewards of this task are only reaped with patience.

It was only last summer that this behavior was first observed. It bears noting that this was not a technique taught to the orangutans by humans (none of whom would be strong enough to pull off the feat). Somehow the rehabilitated orangutans figured this out themselves. As other orangutans have observed the pioneers feast on this hard-to-get-at part of the palm, the behavior has gradually spread.

Russon makes a good case that there is more orangutan tool use than generally believed. This in turn might help explain why orangutans show such technological ingenuity in captivity. Maybe orangutans are using powers they regularly use in the wild without being recognized as doing so by scientists. Well enough and good, but why is it then that chimpanzees, famous for using a wide variety of tools in the wild, are less innovative than orangutans in captivity?

Chimps are certainly smart enough, and are quick to learn to use various tools when taught by humans. But when chimps escape from zoos, it is more likely to be because they figured out how to exploit a weakness in the design of their quarters and got out using athletic skills (as happened at the Dallas Zoo and the Los Angeles Zoo), or through teamwork (as reportedly happened at a zoo in Holland), where one chimp stood on the shoulders of another to reach the top of a wall and then hauled the others up.

The difference between the chimp and the orangutan may be partly temperamental, as suggested above, and partly due to the difference between the reactions to captivity of highly social chimps and more solitary orangutans. Chimps spend some portion of their time in captivity focused on what other chimps are doing and another portion negotiating with their keepers (chimps are keen students of power structures); an orangutan, on the other hand, may spend more of its day appraising its surroundings—"just finding a problem to engage its engineer's brain," as one keeper put it.

In this respect elephants are similar in temperament to orangutans. They are intensely inquisitive, have famously good memories, and apparently love to work on problems. They also have a killer combination of strength and fine motor control that allows them to use their trunk for everything from brute force to lock picking.

Recall the elephant tinkering at Marine World Africa USA. Keepers across the country cite similar feats. Harry Peachey notes that the elephants under his care love to unscrew anything they can lay their trunks on. He remembers back in 1976 when they had to chain the elephants to posts at night in order to protect a young male from a female who would regularly push him into a moat when the keepers weren't around. The chain was secured to the post by a clevis, an iron clasp shaped like the Greek letter omega. An iron rod was inserted through eye holes at the bottom of the omega and then fastened in place by a bolt tightened with a long-handled wrench.

The young bull did not like this restraint one bit, and the keepers would arrive in the mornings to find the elephant roaming free in the enclosure with his leg chain trailing behind him. Using his trunk he would unscrew the bolts, something no human could have achieved without a tool.

Similarly, a female elephant figured out how to unscrew inch-thick iron rods with eye holes that the keepers used to attach bark slabs to the wall of the enclosure (the elephants liked to rub against the bark slabs). The eye rods were secured through a hole in a wall by a bolt that the keepers would tighten with a socket wrench. The female elephant in question would wrap her trunk around the eye part of the rod and use that leverage to untwist the bolt. Peachey also discovered other elephants who would try to unscrew the ends of cables where they were attached to fixtures. All in all there seems to be a lot of unscrewing going on in elephant enclosures around the country.

And in aquariums. Despite the handicap of having flippers rather than hands, dolphins do quite well with the parts of their anatomy they can control. Keepers note that dolphins will use their jaws to unscrew bolts, sometimes bolts that hold the aquarium together. Dolphin behavior authority Diana Reiss notes that dolphins have been observed picking up small objects with their blowholes. They also spit water to move things and can use their jaws to manipulate objects.

Richard Connor, an authority on dolphin behavior, has studied the animals for three decades. He recalls one occasion where he saw a dolphin use another fish as a weapon. The dolphin was trying to flush out an eel. It grabbed a scorpion fish in its mouth, and then, using its rostrum as a probe, inserted the fish into the crevice where the eel was hiding, forcing the eel to come out.

While we are on the subject of devious marine life, electric rays have on occasion demonstrated feeding strategies that seem imaginative, whether the innovation is the product of trial and error encoded in their genes, or true resourcefulness. The connection to tool use is tenuous at best, but the story is too good to ignore. Lou Garibaldi heard the story from John Prescott, curator of the now defunct Marineland of the Pacific. Marineland had a collection of electric rays collected from local California waters. The keepers were somewhat perplexed because they had never seen the rays take food when divers were feeding the rest of the fish. One evening Prescott was working late and watched as a large electric ray swam alongside a spotted grouper. Suddenly the ray administered a shock to the big fish, which promptly regurgitated partially digested fish it had eaten during an earlier feeding. The ray then did an abrupt about face and quickly scarfed up the regurgitated fish. According to Garibaldi, Prescott believed that he was witnessing an adaptation that allowed the relatively slow rays to acquire a meal with a minimum of exertion and a big payoff.

Elephants have more imaginative ways of harassing other animals. At the International Wildlife Park in Grand Prairie, Nebraska, Mimi would hide rocks in her cheeks, and then, when the opportunity presented itself, hurl the rocks at the rhino in the adjacent enclosure. According to Bonnie Hendrickson, it was not clear whether this was all in fun or the result of active dislike. This was not the only elephant who figured out how to use rocks to make a point beyond the confines of his enclosure. According to Harry Peachey of the Columbus Zoo, Koko had a major league arm and control. He also used his skills to good effect.

One of Koko's pet peeves was a trackless train that brought visitors by the elephant enclosure on a regular basis. At one time, the zoo was doing some landscaping, which meant that Koko had access to a nice supply of rocks. These he would regularly hurl at the train with impressive accuracy, according to Peachey. "After he coldcocked a couple of people, we stripped the top three feet of earth away so that he could not get at any more rocks," recalls the veteran keeper. "Then he started spraying the train with water or throwing mud."

Other irritations that might prompt a pachyderm missile or watergun attack included the truck of a visiting vet from Ohio State and crowds of kids hollering his name. Unfortunately for

Koko, kids love to be sprayed with water, so Koko's retaliation would only prompt more irritating cheers.

Elephants are prodigiously strong and can easily kill a human if aroused. Indeed, between 1976 and 1991, there were fifteen elephant-related deaths in the United States, at that time making the job of elephant keeper the single most dangerous occupation in the country. According to OSHA, a keeper had three times the chance of mortal injury than a coal miner. Obviously, an elephant does not need weapons if it wants to do harm. This is what makes the rock throwing interesting.

It is hard to gauge whether Koko had truly malevolent intent with his rock throwing. Elephants are acutely aware of their strength and more likely, he simply wanted to make a point. In any event, elephant rock throwers have figured out a way to project their power when thwarted by steel bars—an event that would not occur in nature. Very clever indeed.

As the elephant stories suggest, there is a very slippery slope between using tools and using tools as weapons. If it is not clear whether Koko intended to cause harm or not, there is less ambiguous evidence of other species who have discovered how to enhance their capacity to hurt other animals. Out of Africa comes striking evidence that a group of wild chimps may be in the process of discovering the potential of weapons.

Chapter Seven

THE ARSENAL OF POWER FROM CLUBS TO SEX

Weapons

Harvard University's anthropology department lies at the top of five flights of fusty wooden stairs in the Peabody Museum of Anthropology and Ethnography on Divinity Avenue in Cambridge. It's an old building, haunted by the incunabala of long lost tribes and the ghosts of an era when anthropologists thought nothing of collecting the accoutrements of ancestor worship, not to mention the bones of the ancestors themselves. As I trudge up to the department, I get a glimpse of a dizzying array of artifacts. Ghosts of the past aside, there is a pleasing ramshackle quality to the collection; you never know what you might find in one of its corners (when a resident anthropologist casually opened a drawer to show a group of visiting scientists from Russia a cast of the remains of "Lucy," a 3-million-year-old hominid discovered by Donald Johanson, one of the group was so overcome she burst into tears). Today, I'm not distracted by either hominid skeletons or scarification masks; I've come to see some sticks.

Some months earlier I visited the forest in Uganda where these sticks originated. There, I saw a few of the victims of beatings with these sticks, and I spoke with witnesses to the attacks. A beating in Africa ordinarily would not prompt a trip from New York to Cambridge, much less Africa, but these attacks were momentous. To a degree, seeing is knowing, and I felt that I needed to see these sticks if I was to begin to understand what had happened in the forests of Uganda.

On the fifth floor I'm met by Carol Hooven, a young-looking, brown-haired graduate student in biological anthropology, and then we join up with Richard Wrangham, one of the world's leading thinkers about chimpanzee behavior, who divides his time between Harvard and the Makare University Biological Field Station in the Kibale Forest in Uganda. We walk up one more flight of stairs to the conservation department, where we find Scott Fulton, who had treated and restored the sticks (some broken during transit from Africa to the US). He leads us into a clean, well-lit work area and pulls out two long, white trays holding a variety of sticks and logs, each tagged with orange plastic tape and a simple description such as, "Stick used as club."

Carol gazes at the sticks thoughtfully. One is like a divining rod, about four feet long with a crook at the end, another is shorter and thicker. Perhaps Carol is thinking back to January 25, 1999. She and a tracker named Donor Muhangyi had been following a group of chimps. Tracking is an essential part of field research, and it is arduous work, requiring that the field workers follow the chimps to the trees where they build their nests at night and then return before dawn if they are to find the chimps before they begin their nomadic foraging during the day. Low to the ground, chimps can simply melt into brush nearly impassable for humans, so even in the best of times, few assistants or researchers see what is going on at every point during the day.

Thus they were lucky to have the chimps in sight at 9:30 that morning. According to her field notes, that is when a male chimp, named Imoso, picked up the long stick with the crook and began beating Outamba, a female chimp in the group. The attack went on for over eight minutes. The violence directed at a female who could not fight back against the big male made her sick at heart, but she was also exhilarated. Trembling, she returned to the camp. At first she was too excited to speak. Settling down, she told Richard Wrangham what she had seen. After listening in stunned silence, Wrangham extended his hand. "Congratulations," he said. "What you observed has never before been seen."

In this blood-drenched corner of Uganda, it is metaphorically apt to imagine that chimps might have picked up the use of weapons from observation—there have been plenty of human examples to imitate. The Kibale Forest lies in Uganda in the foothills of the Rwenzori Mountains, close upon the border of what used to be called Zaire. To the south lies Rwanda, where Hutus slaughtered 800,000 Tutsis in a genocidal uprising in the early 1990s. To the West in Zaire, a civil war still simmers. This conflict followed from a chain reaction of events as Tutsis, backed by Uganda, regained control of Rwanda and drove hundreds of thousands of Hutus into Zaire. In Uganda, several murderous gangs and messianic groups operate in the mountains. Indeed, not long after the attack witnessed by Carol, a band of guerrillas from a group called Interahamwe hacked to death eight tourists and burned to death a Ugandan ranger in the Bwindi Impenetrable Forest to the south.

Apart from homicidal gangs, the region also contains some of the world's most famous primate research stations. There is Karisoke in Rwanda, high in the Virungas, miraculously intact (more about that later in this chapter) nearly forty years after it was established by Dian Fossey as a base to study the world's last remnant populations of mountain gorillas. Lower down the flanks of the volcanoes in Zaire lies Kihusi Viega, a refuge for lowland gorillas. It has suffered as thousands of hungry refugees have periodically encamped nearby, but it has a dedicated cadre of Zairois park guards who have tried to protect the gorillas despite almost complete isolation from supplies

and support. Some of the guards maintained their posts despite the fact that they were not paid for eighteen months during one period in the late 1990s. Further south in Uganda lies
the Bwindi Impenetrable Forest, where various researchers
have studied chimps and gorillas. And then there is Kibale, or
more formally, the Makare University Biological Field Station,
where Carol Hooven and other researchers may be witnessing
the first glimmerings of weapon use in the animal kingdom.

The use of a stick in a beating is a far cry from a rocket-firing
Predator drone. As of this writing there are four confirmed reports of subsequent observations—a very scarce data set—and
there remain open (and fascinating) questions about what was
in the mind of Imoso when he flailed at Outamba. Still, the impact of this observation is stunning. One can't help but think of
the Stanley Kubrick drama based on Arthur C. Clarke's *2001*.
At the beginning of the film, the audience sees a group of
chimplike hominids in rugged, dry terrain. As the strains of
Strauss's *Thus Spake Zarathustra* surge, a chimplike creature
stares at one of the mysterious, metallic monoliths that show
up at various points in the film. Then the hominid seizes a
bone and crashes it on the skull of a long-dead animal. Shortly
thereafter, the ape brings it down on one of the other members
of its group.

It is a powerful scene. Human ingenuity is never more ex-
travagant than when devising tools to kill other humans, and
we wonder at the origin of our dark skills. Still, the amount of
time between the moment when ape men first used tools in
food gathering and when they first used weapons on each
other was probably a good deal longer than a few minutes—
more like hundreds of thousands, if not millions of years.
What Carol and Donor saw in the Kibale forest notwithstand-
ing, early tool use probably had more to do with food gathering than with murder (the chimps in the Tai Forest in the Ivory
Coast have used rocks and sticks to smash open nuts for years,

but have never been observed using these implements on each other). On the other hand, at least for humans, warfare and defense have become drivers of technological innovation.

That is certainly the case today. The research behind many of the technological innovations of the twentieth century, including the harnessing of nuclear power, the development of the Internet, and the invention of the carbon fiber that adds power to your Big Bertha driver, was funded by money intended to develop new instruments of warfare. In a perfect world, it would probably be the other way around, but without defense budgets there likely would be no peace dividends, since voters have proven again and again that they are far more willing to spend money on research for defense than they are for pure research to improve our lives.

So much for humans, but what about animals? Most predators don't need weapons; they are weapons. Nature is very good at equipping animals with an arsenal of tools to inflict grievous injury or death without the help of any technological prosthesis. In the remote Pribilof Islands in the middle of the Bering Sea I've seen male fur seals with huge strips of flesh ripped off during fights with other males. Male tigers regularly die from wounds inflicted during aggressive encounters with other males (if the wound is in a spot where the tiger can't reach with its healing tongue, it will likely become infected, so weakening the tiger than it cannot hunt effectively). Indeed, a good deal of evolutionary ingenuity has gone into the development of greeting, submission, and other rituals that mute the consequences of aggressive encounters within a group. Those few animals that engage in warfare with other groups of their same kind do so without resort to weapons.

Again, they don't need to. Before he established the chimp research program in Kibale in 1988, Wrangham began his work at Jane Goodall's Gombe Stream Reserve. In studies of intergroup raids there he discovered that during warfare chimps show none of the restraint that mute the consequences of fights to improve status inside a group. Sometimes raiding groups will hold an enemy chimp down while others try to rip it apart. (Wrangham argues that this rare natural instance of intraspecies warfare is, for better or worse, one piece of evidence of the extremely close links between humans and chimps. He believes that the shared trait of warfare suggests that human proclivities to wage war predate the dawn of the hominid line. Wrangham develops this argument in *Demonic Males: Apes and the Origins of Human Violence*, which he co-authored with Dale Peterson.) Some studies have shown that as much as one third of all male chimps die at the hands of other chimps. With that kind of kill rate, who needs weapons? Hence I was simply fascinated when Wrangham first told me about what Carol and Donor had seen in the forests of Uganda.

I had run into Wrangham at an interdisciplinary meeting on animal intelligence convened by the Chicago Academy of Sciences in honor of the fortieth anniversary of Jane Goodall's research in the Gombe Stream region of Tanzania. I knew him from interviews conducted during the reporting of my story on apes and humans for *National Geographic*. He was cautious but excited when he told me the news. The caution was merited because of the paucity of data. With such a small data base, the behavior might be the product of anything, including happenstance. Still, as soon as he told me, I knew I had to get to Kibale.

It was a year before the opportunity arose, but when it did, I pounced. I was doing some editorial consulting with the United Nations Development Agency on a series of papers on desertification. Given an onerous deadline, they offered to fly me to their headquarters at the UN compound outside Nairobi to finish up the project. This offer came up on a Tuesday, and I flew out the next evening. During my blizzard of preparations I found the time to call Richard and ask whether I might stop by Kibale on my way home from Nairobi a week later. He graciously agreed, giving me the names of the key people at the station. As for directions, he might have been guiding me to the local Starbucks: "Get to Fort Portal," he said as though this was the easiest thing in the world, "and find the cab stand near the post office. They all know the way, and the trip takes about forty-five minutes." This was not a lot to go on, but then I did not have the time to worry about that.

After I finished up in Nairobi, I took the short flight to Entebbe, arriving at the Grand Imperial Hotel in Kampala at about midnight (the hotel's name was quite accurate, since the sprawling building clearly had seen its best days when Uganda was part of the British empire). My plan was to get up early, hire a reliable car and driver, and head out that morning. To get to Fort Portal, we would have to traverse the entire width of the country, but Richard had said the trip could be done in six to eight hours. Hopefully, I would arrive in Fort Portal before sunset; hopefully, we could get directions to the research site; and hopefully, Kathi Pieta, who ran the chimp station, would not turn me away (I'd sent an e-mail, but Richard had said that the staff only collected e-mails intermittently, when they made trips into town).

Then my plan was to get up early and tag along if someone was planning to follow the chimps. I've visited most of the major great ape research stations over the years and am fairly familiar with the etiquette of following chimps, gorillas, bonobos, and orangutans in the wild. After interviewing as many of the researchers and field assistants as I could fit into this short schedule, I planned to have my hypothetically reliable driver pick me up and take me back to Kampala. I had to squeeze the trip, because, faced with a plethora of deadlines, I had to get back to the United States.

The plan contained more ifs than Rudyard Kipling's poem of that name, and enough hope to loft a dirigible. In fact it was preposterous. In a country where reliable cars are as rare as rhinoceroses, where the roads have one of the worst accident rates in the world, and where you never know what various armed guerrilla groups are going to do, I was leaving myself no margin for error. It would have been absurd to try to limit myself to one day's reporting had this research station been in the Catskills, but it was halfway around the planet in one of the more remote corners of Africa.

Sometimes you have a feeling about these things, though, and when my plane landed in Entebbe without incident, I was off to a good start. The feeling continued the next morning when the hotel concierge found me a car and affable driver who said that he could take me across the country and back for a reasonable fee plus gas (I asked the driver his name several times, but he was so shy and his accent so thick that I only heard a murmur that sounded like Marcel). I took a long look at his rundown Toyota. It seemed okay, and indeed, but for a persistent and ultimately maddening pinging that accompanied us all nine hundred kilometers of the trip, the car ran fine.

"Marcel" said that the direct road between Kampala and Fort Portal was bad, so we took a circuitous route that took us south to Mbarra and then up through Kasese. Once outside of Kampala we did not encounter one traffic light during the entire trip. Indeed, Marcel kept the speedometer needle pressed close to 120 kilometers per hour except on those occasions when we passed through villages. Then he dropped to 100 kilometers per hour.

If Uganda vies for superlatives in any category in Africa, it has the best shot at the title for the most dangerous roads. The problem is that they are good enough to encourage extreme high-speed driving. On the other hand, there are no traffic controls whatsoever. During my trip to Kibale, 3.3 percent of the nation's sportswriters were killed in just one head-on collision, according to the *Monitor*, a lively tabloid. The only real limit on the death toll seems to be the price of gas, which keeps most vehicles off the road. As it was, most of the cars we encountered seemed to be official vehicles of one of the myriad organizations attempting to better the lives of Ugandans.

In the 1970s, I wrote a book entitled *The Alms Race* about the impact of aid money on Africa, and I have since made many trips through the continent. All too often it's a depressing experience and this was no exception. Arrayed along the road were village after village, indistinguishable from the villages I passed on my first trip to East Africa in 1974. The only difference is that there are more villages and fewer forests. Indeed, apart from the foothills of the Rwenzori Mountains, the only significant patch of forest we encountered in two traversals of the country (we took a different route coming back) was along an unpaved and rutted stretch between Butiti and Mubende. This might or might not be coincidence, but it's a relatively safe wager that with the paving of this stretch now well underway, these patches will likely disappear as well.

Much of Africa, including Uganda, has managed the trick of having growth without development. In recent years, Uganda has been applauded for its enlightened government and refreshing willingness to try to bootstrap the economy. Still, what Uganda has proven best at producing is more Ugandans. Otherwise, there is little or nothing that Uganda produces that, at the moment, cannot be produced better or cheaper elsewhere.

If there is one overwhelming asset to the country, it is the physical beauty and gaudy wildlife of its western region. Queen Elizabeth Park, the Kyambura Wildlife Preserve, Rwenzori National Park, Kibale National Park, all could someday produce hard currency and employment if poachers don't kill every animal off and squatters don't cut every tree. The potential rewards of preservation aren't trivial.

Before the genocide, Karisoke and gorilla tourism was the

third largest earner of foreign exchange in neighboring Rwanda. Bill Webber and Amy Vetter helped start ecotourism in the Virungas, and thank God they did. The knowledge that gorillas are worth vastly more alive than they are dead helps explain why mountain gorilla populations increased by ten percent during the 1990s, even as humans slaughtered each other by the hundreds of thousands. To Uganda's east in Kenya, tourism usually vies with coffee exports as the biggest source of hard currency. With almost no infrastructure and a bevy of guerrilla groups marauding in the mountains, tourism—eco or otherwise—is still some years off in Uganda's beautiful mountains.

I had no idea where we were going and neither did my driver, so we started asking for directions in Kasese, seventy kilometers to the south of Fort Portal. As it turned out, however, Wrangham's suggestion did the trick. When we got to run-down Fort Portal, we found plenty of cabbies who knew the station, but none who could explain how to get there. Everybody kept saying "turn right up ahead," but we suspected it was more complicated than that. We took the expedient of hiring a kid on a motorcycle to lead the way.

We arrived just as the sun was setting. I gave my driver some money for a room and meal in Fort Portal, and then introduced myself to the staff. At the compound were Kathi Pieta, who ran the station while she was completing her studies for the University of Vienna, and Kim Duffy, who was doing research as part of her graduate work at UCLA. Naturally, they had no idea I was coming, but to my relief, they knew who I was from my earlier writings on apes and were quite hospitable. At Wrangham's suggestion I came bearing gifts—some food and, more importantly, wine.

In terms of amenities, the camp itself was in the mid-range of research stations I've visited. The buildings were solid, the latrines well designed, and there was even water for washing up.

We enjoyed dinner out on the camp's simple porch. The camp cook had died two weeks earlier of AIDS, so Kathi worked up a nice meal of rice and sauce spiced up by some sardines I had brought along, accompanied by a Wente Cabernet Sauvignon. Kim, fighting some tropical bug, passed on the food, but joined the conversation as the two graduate students told me a bit about the Kanyawara community of chimps.

The group consists of about fifty chimps, including about ten adult males, seventeen mothers in three different geographic groupings, and assorted other infants, adolescent males and non-reproducing females. The Kanyawara chimps don't seem to hunt as much as other chimps in the region, but they will go after red colobus monkeys when the opportunity presents itself.

Further up the mountain slopes lies the Ngogo Primate Project, run by John Mitani of the University of Michigan and David Watts, who began his work with primates at Karisoke. Hunting figures far more prominently in the Ngogo chimp community, with prey that includes black and white colobus, mangabeys, duiker (tiny, deerlike ungulates), and red tail monkeys, as well as red colobus. (The Ngogo chimps apparently also have epic confrontations with neighboring chimp communities, with up to forty male chimps squaring off against each other in battle.)

In the Kanyawara community, Imoso was then the top dog. Described as young and very aggressive, he had grabbed the top spot in 1998 when the former alpha male, Big Brown, found himself hampered by a snare caught on one hand that forced him to carry around a big log until he eventually got free of the wire. Imoso does not seem to be a popular leader, either among the chimps or their human observers.

His reputation did not improve with the discovery that he was a wife beater. As Carol later described the attack during my visit to Harvard, Imoso had been trying to get at Outamba's infant. Perhaps afraid that Imoso intended harm (there have been cases of infanticide in the Kanyawara community), Outamba fended off his efforts to get at the baby. This seemed to enrage Imoso, who began kicking and punching Outamba, who exposed her back to Imoso while she cradled and protected the infant.

Carol took notes in her nice, precise handwriting, and then prepared a summary of the attack for Richard Wrangham. Here is how Carol described what happened next:

> "MS [Imoso] first attacks OU [Outamba] with one stick for about forty-five seconds, holding it with his right hand, near the middle of the stick. She was hit about five times with the stick. My notes read that he beat her 'hard.' (The stick was bought down on her in a somewhat inefficient way—if I were to hit someone with a stick, I'd raise a bent arm, holding the stick at an angle to the object I was hitting, and swing the stick down. MS seemed to start with the stick almost parallel to their body and bring it down in a parallel motion. There was a slight angle to his motion, but not the way a human would do it for maximum impact.) During this first beating, she was also punched and kicked several times."

After resting for a minute, Imoso resumed the beating, this time with two sticks, again held toward the middle of the stick. This continued with Imoso hurting Outamba in a number of creative ways, once hanging from a branch above her and stamping on her with his feet. To Carol, the attack was "interminable." Throughout the beating, Outamba protected the infant, and toward the end, her three-year-old son Tenkere gallantly rushed to her aid, pounding on Imoso's back with his little fists.

Imoso may have started a new fad in Kanyawara. Johnny, his best friend, was the next to beat up poor Outamba. Kathi

witnessed Johnny's attack along with Donor and Amy Pokemp-
ner, a graduate student at the Stony Brook campus of the State
University of New York. This beating took place in July 2000,
during the fruiting season of the uvaropsis trees, a favorite
food of the chimp community. Again, Outamba's infant
daughter Kilimi seemed to figure in the attack. Kathi was observing Outamba, when, seemingly for no reason, Johnny attacked Kilimi. Outamba turned to help her offspring,
whereupon Johnny turned on her. He tried to hit her, and immediately she became submissive.

Johnny was not to be appeased, however, and first he
stepped on her, and then he picked up a big stick and started
hitting her. "He was definitely trying to hit her," says Kathi. "It
wasn't just flailing or accidental. He used an up-and-down motion." Excited by the commotion, two other young males, Mak-
ouko and Kakama came galloping over displaying, at which
point Outamba grabbed her opportunity to escape and fled to
a tree.

The whole attack took maybe three minutes. After a couple
of minutes in the tree, Outamba came down and acceded to
Johnny's invitation to copulate. He left the stick on the forest
floor. After the chimps moved on, Kathi picked up the stick,
and it too is now at the Museum of Anthropology at Harvard.

After the encounter, the humans were stunned, knowing
they had seen something unique, but again, not quite sure
what it meant. You don't launch a study on two sightings, but
the researchers did start paying attention to the ways in which
chimps used sticks.

They have so far documented four attacks. In a couple of
cases, the attacks have come close together, as though one attack plants the idea in another chimp's mind. One day after
Johnny attacked Outamba, another male attacked a female, and
the next day some juveniles threw sticks at another juvenile.

I was to learn more about the niceties of sticks as weapons

when I got up at 4:45 to meet up with Kathi, Donor, and another tracker, Francis Mugurousi, to go in search of Johnny, Imoso, and their battered wives. We left at 5:30 and after a vigorous walk we got to the area of a fruiting ficus tree where the chimps had built their nests the previous evening. At 6:30 we heard the first pant hooting and by 6:50 the chimps were already feeding in the ficus down the trail.

There was Johnny, as well as Mokoko, and a number of other chimps. Imoso, who had not been seen for several months, was not around. As we watched, a little three-year-old female was struggling to get up into the ficus. The trunk at the base was far too large for her to grab, so first she tried climbing a neighboring sapling. Drat, the gap was too big, so she carefully jumped to another closer tree. No luck here either, so the determined toddler tried a third tree. Success! She managed to transfer from a branch of this sapling to a part of the ficus trunk that she could grab. Donor applauded. He is a good-humored man who clearly is very fond of the animals he tracks.

Donor and Francis have "urine sticks" with them, sticks with an absorbent sponge on top that they use to get urine samples from leaves when the chimps above pee. The samples are used for monitoring hormone levels. After retrieving one such sample, I asked Donor for his thoughts on why Imoso had attacked Outamba. Donor's answer: "Imoso is just a mean chimp." He added that he knew he was witnessing something extraordinary when he saw the beating, but his excitement was tempered by his sympathy for poor Outamba. Like Carol, Donor mentioned that the chimp's hitting stroke was not particularly efficient. "It was not like a man hitting another with a stick," said Donor.

While all the instances thus far observed have involved males hitting females, Francis and others have observed male chimps threaten other males with sticks. Francis noted that one male named Stocky was attacked by Johnny in 1998. After screaming, Stocky picked up a one-meter-long stick. Seeing this, Johnny stopped his attack and ran into a tree. On another occasion, during a charge Imoso picked up a half-meter-long stick and threw it at another male named Tofu. He missed.

The attacks raise many more questions than answers. Is this a brand-new behavior, or the first observation of something that has gone on for thousands of years? Why is it that chimps seem to use sticks more on females than males? Is it because the stick as weapon is a new technology and the risks are lower trying it out on females, who are no physical match for the males? When I spoke to him on my return to the US, Richard Wrangham noted that male-male attacks have such high stakes that few males would chance the risk of trying out a weapon before they were certain that it would work.

On the other hand, who knows what chimps do during the ninety-nine percent of the time that they are out of sight of humans. If they ever develop an efficient swing, the chimps, with their incredible strength, could do real damage to each other and to other species. Richard also said that only one out of one hundred sticks might be robust enough to withstand a blow delivered by an adult male chimp.

After a while, the chimps moved off. We followed, Kathi occasionally jotting something down in her notebook. The blond graduate student had a diffident manner, but she moved with easy confidence in the forest, and didn't miss a thing. We had not gone far when the chimps simply melted into the thick undergrowth, providing an excellent demonstration of the virtues of knuckle-walking in such an area. As they disappeared on what seemed like a very deliberate route, I asked Kathi which of the chimps makes the plan for the day. "Johnny thinks he does," she said with a laugh.

The preliminary evidence of weapon use may send a thrill of excitement up the spine, but the last thing these and other chimps need is a new way to hasten their own extinction. The

Kanyawara chimps have plenty of external threats to cope with right now. A shadowy guerrilla group called the ADF is in the region. No one seems to know what they are fighting or why, but they have terrorized the region with their predilection for rape, torture, mutilation, and gruesome dismemberments. Indeed, Carol and other foreign researchers were evacuated after one set of killings, when the authorities heard rumors that the ADF was using loggers as spies to identify the whereabouts of whites in the region.

Then there are poachers who set snares to catch whatever comes along. Even if a chimp gets free of the wire, they often lose a hand. One chimp, Nectar, eventually lost both hands and starved when she could no longer climb, according to Kathi. The station now has two full-time employees dedicated to finding and destroying snares.

After failing to reestablish contact with Johnny and his chimp gang, we made our way back to the station. There I talked some more with Kim Duffy and with other trackers who stopped by. Then my driver arrived and, accompanied by the incessant pinging in his car, we made our way, at insane speed, back to Kampala.

Back in New York, exhausted, having flown straight from Entebbe, I have that inevitable sense of relief that comes from leaving an impoverished, disease-ravaged region that bears the scars of war and returning to the relative safety and comfort of my home just outside New York City. The date is September 8, 2001. Three days later, as I drive my son Alec to nursery school, we hear a bulletin that a plane has crashed into the World Trade Center. As we are listening, the second plane hits the second tower. My son, who is three and three quarters, asks, "Is the plane going to be all right, Daddy?" Completely lost as to how to shield a three-year-old from the enormity of what has just happened, I choose my words carefully and simply say, "I don't think so." We humans have ways of killing ourselves that chimps could never imagine.

Or, perhaps, want to imagine. The thought occurs to me later when I again ponder the mysteries of the stick-wielding chimps of Kibale: Why sticks? Why not rocks? Chimps use rocks to smash nuts. At Gombe chimps have used rocks in hunting. In one documented instance, a male threw a rock at an adult forest pig in order to separate it from a piglet the chimps were hunting. A chimp could mortally injure another chimp by hitting it with a rock.

Both Wrangham and Hooven speculate that this might be one reason chimps use sticks rather than rocks: they intend to inflict hurt rather than injury. Most of the attacks have been directed at sexually active females, and while the males might intend harm to the babies, they have nothing to gain by killing their mates. Brutal as it seems, is it possible that the use of sticks is an indicator of restraint rather than a chimp arms race?

It's also possible that chimps are more familiar with sticks. They use them occasionally to scratch themselves, and, more to the point, they will sometimes throw sticks at mangabeys to chase them away from fruits that the chimps covet. I had chimps throw branches at me in the Ndoki Forest in the Congo, but this was clearly for show as the branches fell harmlessly to the ground. Chimps also use sticks as props during threat displays. A male wants to look as big and threatening as possible during a threat, and he will seize on anything to make himself look and sound more formidable. (One equally fascinating development observed since the first attack has been instances in which young females carry around sticks. In this case, however, the females hold the sticks more like dolls than weapons, sometimes even placing them in little nests. Could it be that these young females are using sticks as symbolic representations of babies?)

Perhaps the use of weapons grew out of threat behavior, but there are many other possibilities. Carol wonders whether Imoso might have gotten the idea from farmers who have invaded the park and who brandish sticks and machetes at the chimps when they stage crop raids. Wrangham doubts this, but whatever the origins, Uganda is a fitting locale for the first observation of a primate using a weapon against one of its own.

Chimps will use a wide variety of weapons if the opportunity presents itself. I learned of one such incident when I received a letter following the publication of *The Parrot's Lament*. In 1978, when Nancy Hartwell of Maryland was working as administrative director at Socomac, a port services company in Duala, Cameroon, the personnel manager, a local named Emmanuel Ebaa'a, told her of an unfortunate incident involving his uncle and a chimpanzee who turned out to have a touch of Daniel Boone in her makeup. The uncle was hunting in the forests of southern Cameroon one day armed with a rifle. When he came upon a female chimpanzee and her infant, he decided to give the two a wide berth and started climbing a tree. Later, with great embarrassment, he had to tell the emergency room doctor how he had ended up with a gunshot wound. In his haste to climb the tree, he had dropped the rifle. The mom chimp picked it up, looked at it, cocked it, pointed it at him and shot him in the leg. I have not been able to reach Ebaa'a and so offer this story without comment.

Other apes have used sticks and logs as weapons, but most of the apes observed doing so have been in captivity, or have spent some time in captivity. Ann Russon says that male orangutans will sometimes try to topple dead trees or large branches on top of people, and that they have pretty good aim. Ken Gold, a primatologist from Chicago, recalls that when he was at the Apenheul Monkey Park in Holland, a group of bonobos used sticks as weapons. A peacock had wandered into the bonobos' enclosure and, despite threats by the bonobos, did not get the message that the bonobos were inviting the peacock to leave. One of the bonobos then went into its cage, got a stick, and killed the peacock.

This example of bonobo violence is something of a surprise, since a very long time ago bonobos discovered that sex was a far more powerful weapon than any mere stick, or even the most advanced weaponry of modern society. If weapons might be defined as physical attributes or technologies that serve to gain and maintain power, then no invention of ape or humanity can hold a candle to the power shift that has occurred through the differences in sexual behavior of bonobos (*Pan paniscus*) and their close relatives the chimpanzee (*Pan troglodytes*). Over a period of about 1.5 million years, the different role that sex plays in bonobo society has been accompanied by anatomical changes that have profoundly altered the male-female balance of power.

Through anatomical and hormonal changes that made female bonobos more available for sex, the females completely reversed the power structure of typical great ape societies. If chimp society has a tendency to use force to keep females in a subordinate position, bonobo societies have gone in the opposite direction. Many women who feel marginalized by the old boy network might envy the situation of a bonobo female, in which she has seniority during the business of the day. In another reversal, males have no obvious hierarchy, while females develop alliances and confer status on their male offspring. If chimps provide a behavioral analogy for the human proclivity for warfare, bonobos have several other traits similar to humans in the sexual realm, such as face-to-face mating and a tendency for copulation and sex that is not directly related to reproduction.

Until recently, not much was known about bonobos at all. They are the newest ape; only identified as a separate species in 1933. Isolated from other chimp species by the Congo river, bonobos (the name probably comes from a misspelling of Bolobo, a village in the Congo) split from chimps between 1.5 and 2.5 million years ago. Some years ago I visited the research station in Wamba, Zaire, run by the Japanese primatologist Takayoshi Kano. When you first see bonobos in the wild, there is the initial shock of seeing animals walking around relatively upright and mating face-to-face. Inevitably the question arises: Are these graceful creatures our closest relatives? More likely, however, the behavioral similarities to humans result from ecology rather than close ancestry.

Bonobos tend to gather in large groups, sometimes containing as many as one hundred members or more. It is unclear whether bonobos have such large groups because they need to or because they can, but whatever the reason, what other apes settle through aggressive encounters, bonobos settle through sex.

Most chimp females are only available for copulation when they comes into estrus, for a few days during the animal's forty-six-day menstrual cycle. Bonobo females, by contrast, are either in estrus, or false estrus, and available for sex for nearly half their cycle. Sex or simulated sex has become the currency of all social relationships; it's handed out like confetti to all comers. Females rub genitals with other females as a tension-lessening/greeting ceremony, males do false matings with other males for the same reason—adults with children, and every other conceivable permutation. Make that inconceivable, since the better part of bonobo sex does not result in orgasm or pregnancy.

With females several times more available to copulate than their nearby chimp cousins, males don't need to compete for access. There is also less reason to form alliances, less reason to raid other groups for females, less reason to get as big as possible, less reason to develop martial skills, less reason to do anything stressful at all. Males have essentially been domesticated by females.

All of these factors have reduced the physical disparity between males and females. Indeed, one characteristic of bonobo society is that the species is paedomorphic, meaning that its members carry a number of physical traits associated with childhood into adulthood. Compared with chimps, they are more gracile, the males have less prominent brow ridges, and both sexes spend more time walking upright. Their vocalizations are higher than chimps', and, according to Frans de Waal, males will engage in a dialogue during antagonistic encounters, something never seen in chimps thus far.

Among other things, the differences between bonobos and chimps show how seemingly small changes can have large effects in a relatively short period of time. Bonobos evolved in the very heart of the Congo basin rain forest, a refugium relatively insulated from the climatic reverberations of the ice ages, which periodically inflicted periods of cooling and drying on more outlying areas of the ecosystem. In many cases they live just a few miles from their cousins *Pan troglodytes*, but, isolated by the great river, they took their own evolutionary path. To paraphrase a remark by de Waal, with chimps, power is a means of getting sex; with bonobos, sex is a means of getting power.

The question remains: What launched bonobos on their different path? As is the case with so many things in nature, the answer may be as simple as ecology. While chimps and bonobos live in forests that are virtually identical in flora on the two sides of the Congo river, there is one major difference. North of the Congo River chimps share their habitat with gorillas, who feast on ground vegetation; south of the river bonobos have both the trees and the ground cover to themselves.

Wrangham argues that the bonobos' ability to eat and walk might be the difference between peace and war, between the free-loving bonobos and the sexually competitive and sexually coercive chimps of East Africa. For chimps, says Wrangham, the key to success is to hurry from fruiting tree to fruiting tree. Those who hesitate or linger on the way tend to lose out by being late to the table. This forces the chimps to break into smaller groups, with the males moving rapidly from feeding site to feeding site. Bonobos, on the other hand, can stop and eat the daisies, with less pressure either to move quickly or separate from the main group.

How does this relate to sex? One possibility now under investigation is whether in a larger group frequent sexual liaisons with many males protect infants, because males, who sometimes kill infants of rivals to bring females back into estrus, don't know whether or not they might be killing their own offspring. As Wrangham put it, "The ideal might be for the female to make herself mildly attractive for a long period of time." Where competition with gorillas or other factors make the environment more sparse, females don't want to attract a lot of males around them, notes Wrangham, so their response has been to have a super-attractive estrus for a very short period of time. The downside of this, says Wrangham, is that it can lead to coerced sex—the kind of sex Wrangham's colleagues witnessed after the beating of various females.

The stingier pickings in many chimp environments may also help explain chimp warfare. Long-term studies of chimp warfare at Gombe suggest that chimp conflicts are primarily fights over territory and only secondarily do they use raids to kidnap other females. The females in a chimp band benefit from these raids, however, because with more resources they breed more frequently and their offspring do better.

For better or worse, warfare puts a premium on brainpower. Many calculations go into whether to pick a fight with another band and how to proceed. Wrangham's research suggests that chimps will attack when they have a strong sense of numerical superiority (which might explain why chimps are pretty good at learning numbers in captivity).

Once a fight begins, someone needs to deploy the troops. Christophe Boesch has studied chimp battles in the Tai Forest. Among other things he has observed that a group might have one leader for food gathering or hunting and a different leader during conflict. For many years the chairman of the joint chiefs of staff in Tai was a male Christophe had named Brutus. Even as he aged, Boesch said that Brutus continued to influence battle strategy from the rear echelons. Boesch observed that the younger males would look back to Brutus, perhaps for reassurance, perhaps for guidance, as a battle escalated.

Clearly there are other evolutionary advantages to intelligence, since bonobos are as bright or brighter than chimps and they have chosen the path of peace. On the other hand, Wrangham argues that there are some compelling pieces of evidence supporting the links between ecology and sexual availability. In the Tai Forest, where there are no gorillas and relatively rich food sources on the ground, Christophe Boesch has discovered that female chimps come into estrus or false estrus almost as frequently as bonobos. While in East Africa chimps might come into estrus swellings between four and ten times in the five- or six-year interval between births, bonobos might have thirty-four months of swellings during that same interval. The figure for the Tai females is thirty-six to thirty-nine months, several times the frequency of other chimps and roughly the same as bonobos. Other bonobolike attributes of the Tai chimps are that the females seem to form alliances and that the groups are relatively stable.

On the other hand, the Tai chimps do regularly go to war with other chimp bands, a much more chimplike than bonobolike behavior. These contradictory facts might be reconciled by ecology too, however. While relatively rich, the Tai

Forest has become an island as deforestation in West Africa has destroyed most of the area's original rain forests. With no new lands to colonize, chimps must compete with each other when chimp populations grow.

What can we make of weapon use? The behavior is new and unfolding. Even the word "weapon" has to be qualified, since there are still many unknowns about the intent of the chimps using the sticks to hit others. The exciting possibility at Kibale is that observers may be witnessing the discovery and dissemination of a new technology in a chimp group, offering the possibility of witnessing how new behaviors become integrated into a culture.

William McGrew, who has devoted much of his work to the study of chimp culture, sets certain criteria for a behavior to be considered cultural. He argues that cultural behaviors are collective—"this is the way we do it"—they are group-typical, they are transmitted by social learning, both from old to young and across age groups, and they bind a group together, among other factors. The Kibale chimps ought to be embarrassed if it turns out that the thing they bind together the males is wife-beating with sticks. More likely, if this behavior continues through generations, it will represent an emerging custom, in the way that termite-fishing with twigs is a custom at Gombe, and as such perhaps represent a component of a culture. Whatever it turns out to be, this novel use of sticks offers an opportunity to watch chimp minds in the process of discovery.

The researchers at Kibale continue to collect data on these attacks. There are so many open questions that Wrangham and Hooven are still trying to figure out how to interpret this new behavior, although they plan to present a preliminary description of their discovery to the scientific community in the near future. For her part, Carol was sufficiently struck by her encounters with the Kanyawara chimps that she has decided to explore the role of testosterone in behavior as a direction for her research.

Back at the Peabody Museum, I watch as Scott Fulton puts the sticks away. There is nothing special about them, really. Some approach the size of logs, while others look like they would break with a strong blow. The chimps apparently have not figured out how to select the optimum stick for beating (chimps at Gombe seem to know the characteristics that make for a good termite-fishing twig), and according to Carol, Kathi, Donor and others, they don't yet use a grip that would make for a more efficient blow. Still, there is a horrifying magic to these primitive weapons. One of three-million-year-old Lucy's ancestors probably used something similar. There is also a perfect aptness to the fact that they will someday be on display at the Peabody, devoted to the the many, various, and ancient expressions of human nature.

Chapter Eight

WHEN ELEPHANTS CHEAT

Deception

We are at our best intellectually when we are doing our worst. Think about the massive deception mounted by the failed energy giant Enron to convince stock market analysts, regulators, and the public that the company was more profitable than it turned out to be. It took far more intellectual firepower to concoct the intricate network of partnerships that allowed the energy company to maintain this fiction than it would have taken to offer a simple and straightforward accounting of profits and losses, assets and liabilities.

Enron's managers expended this effort (and managed to enlist others in its conspiracy) because, at least in the short run, deception pays. Creatures great and small have experimented individually and collectively with less pernicious forms of this lesson (deception that fools a predator that wants to eat you is different than deception that steals from a colleague who is essential to the success of your career). If you are a caterpillar it pays to have a bird think you are a snake; if you are a cuckoo it pays to have another bird think your eggs are its own and raise your offspring.

Huge numbers of creatures practice deception, but most don't know that they do it. The leafy sea dragon from southwest Australia is a sea horse that looks for all the world like a

floating bit of seaweed. It's a clever disguise, since the creatures that eat sea horses typically don't eat floating seaweed,
and the creatures that eat floating seaweed are not interested in
eating leafy sea dragons (although they may occasionally make
a terrible dietary faux pas). The leafy sea dragon probably does
not know that it looks like a piece of seaweed. Sometime in the
distant past a chance mutation left some ancestral sea horse
with a feathery appendage that confused enough predators so
that those sea horses with such accoutrements had a better
chance to survive and breed. When they bred with other leafy-
appendaged sea horses, their offspring did even better. Evolution is akin to creating a portrait by doing ten thousand
canvases and then having voracious critics eat the ones that
don't scare them off. By combining the elements of the better
likenesses, the portrait becomes more and more refined. Eventually you have a sea horse that looks exactly like a piece of
seaweed, an octopus that can mimic the coloration and texture
of the sea floor, and a caterpillar that looks for all the world
like the head of a fierce snake.

Then there are deceptions rooted in behavior, e.g. the
plover that feigns a broken wing to lead predators away from a
nest. Though artful, such deceptions are often rooted in the
genes rather than individual genius. Even where an animal
does appear to invent a deception, as, for instance, when a dog
limps to get petted, the reasoning might simply be: "If I do this,
he'll do that," rather than, "If I can convince the boss I'm hurt,
he'll be nicer to me."

Then there are cases that involve the conscious planting of a
false belief. During World War II, the allies let the Germans
discover a body they had planted off the coast of Spain.
Among the dead man's belongings was a briefcase carrying
"secret" messages suggesting that the Allies planned to launch
their invasion of Europe in Greece. The reasoning behind this
was that the Germans were more likely to believe this disinfor-

mation if they had to work to disguise and interpret the messages themselves. Similarly, the Allies sacrificed a number of troops in surprise attacks even though the enemy knew about the plans in advance. They did so because they did not want the Germans to know that they had broken their most secret codes.

Both these famous cases show the enormous advantage of being able to manipulate a rival's state of mind—not just knowledge but emotions. If you know what your rival thinks he knows, and how strongly he believes in what he knows, you can reinforce or change those beliefs to your advantage. Humans have been doing this for over one hundred thousand years, and we are pretty good at it; *decipio ergo cogito* might be an apt rephrasing of Descartes's formulation.

Before we can manipulate another's mental state, however, we have to be aware that others have mental states. With a little help from Daniel Dennett, David Premack, a psychologist at the University of Pennsylvania, figured out a way to test this. Based on the notion of a Punch and Judy show, the experiment goes like this: The researcher presents a tableau in which a child watches a stage with a box and a bag on a table. As the audience watches, a little girl named Sally enters a room and puts a marble in the box. Then she leaves the room. While she is out, Ann enters the room and moves the marble from the box to the bag, then leaves the room. Once she is gone, Sally re-enters the room. The question is: where will Sally look for the marble?

Very young children watching this little pantomime will point to the bag because that is where the marble is. Once children are four or so, however, they realize that Sally has the false belief that the marble is in the box. In other words, they are aware of Sally's state of mind; they are aware that others are conscious; they are aware that others can be mistaken; they are aware that others can be deceived. They are on their way to understanding, if not devising, the ruses that nations and individuals have perpetrated on each other since the dawn of the species.

Since I've promised to introduce surprising animals in this chapter, I might as well start with children (I know a number of parents who vigorously insist that there is little distinction between children and animals for the first few years). Anyway, with two experimental subjects readily at hand in the form of my two youngest children, I decided to try out the Sally/Ann test myself, enlisting the aid of our babysitter, Lera, and my wife, Mary. We scheduled the experiment for November 10, 2000, when Sofia had just turned four and Alec was two-and-three-quarters years old. Conducting the experiment turned out to be a little embarrassing because Alec and Sofia got so excited that they started telling everyone, including their nursery school teachers, that "Daddy's going to experiment on us!" I half expected dour-faced enforcers from Child Welfare to show up at the front door.

Instead of a marble, we used a potato. As Sofia and Alec watched, Lera put the potato in a bag and left the room. Then Mary entered and put the potato in a covered basket and left the room. The first subject was Alec. To be scientific, I decided to measure the subject. I did this by holding him upside down by his feet. Once he was rightside-up again and his giggles had subsided, we commenced the little show. Afterwards, when we asked where Lera would look for the potato, Alec said, "Look in the basket," dutifully exemplifying the limited consciousness of his age cohort. Sofia, on the other hand, hesitated a long time before answering, and then, seemingly realizing Lera's false belief, said, "In the bag."

Case closed. Or is it? Perhaps my wording was not careful enough. It is easy to see how a child under three could confuse the question, "Where will Lera look for the potato," with

"Where should Lera look for the potato." So it goes with experiments. Of course, I make no pretense that my attempt was the least bit scientific, but being scientific doesn't seem to help much, either. As many a chastened experimenter has discovered, it is easy to pick at any attempt to replicate this simple tableau with animals.

Moreover, translated into nonlinguistic form, variations of this experiment have been tried with animals many times. Some of the results have been fairly compelling, providing suggestive evidence that some chimps or orangutans understand the mental states of others, but none have been bulletproof. The same frustration that sapped the initial enthusiasm for the language experiments and the mirror test for self-consciousness now seems to be miring this once-promising idea for demonstrating consciousness.

Rather than enter another messy debate, scientists such as Ann Russon eschew discussions of consciousness, and prefer to focus on issues like metacognition, levels of complexity in thought, and reflecting about one's own thinking. Russon looks for evidence that orangutans have thought about their own thinking and then modified their thinking.

For instance, she has looked at some examples of pretending, a phenomenon that has been the subject of a large number of psychological studies. Simple pretending involves behaving as if something is real when it is not. Complex pretending, on the other hand, involves a number of more sophisticated cognitive factors. Among other things, psychologists have asserted that during complex pretending the deceiver maintains two distinct representations of the same situation, one literal and real and the other distorted and imaginary. The pretender must also be able to mark the pretend representation as different from the real situation, and in some cases, scientists require that for an act to qualify as complex pretending the pretense situation must be symbolic in some form, whether that means involving imaginary objects or having multiple representations of the same object.

This is the type of pretense a poker player might maintain during a bluff when, through his body language as he bets, he tries to convey that he has a flush with three hearts showing. This is an example of metacognition in quintessential human form. Let's see how it translates into orangutan poker.

Among the examples that Ann Russon cites is one that involved an orangutan named Princess, a semi-permanent resident at Camp Leakey in Borneo, where she had been raised since infancy. Camp Leakey was established in 1971 by Birute Galdikas near Tanjung Puting in southern Borneo. As Russon reports the incident, Princess, highly socialized to humans and a favorite with visitors, was passing time with a group of people on a bunkhouse porch one afternoon. After a while, she left, as orangutans will, by climbing up the walls and then walking up the roof. On this occasion though, instead of continuing on into the trees, she paused out of sight for several minutes and then reappeared on the porch and was especially sweet and attentive. Moreover, instead of leaving for her evening meal, she stayed on the porch and went to sleep on the doorstep instead of making her nest. As they left for dinner at 6:30, the departing humans had to step over the peacefully sleeping orangutan.

The reason became apparent shortly after the group returned. Princess was asleep on the floor of the bunkhouse and the door was locked with a sliding bar. Roused by the commotion of the residents outside, Princess woke up and groggily slid the bar back, letting her friends inside. Once Princess left, the residents surveyed the bunkhouse. Upstairs they discovered that she had rummaged through their suitcases, liberally availing herself of food and treats the visitors had been saving for special occasions. They also discovered that the screen near the peak of the roof was torn, offering access to an agile thief.

Russon surmises that Princess saw the torn screen as she was exiting by the roof in the afternoon, and then hastily revised her plans. What is noteworthy is that she maintained the two representations of reality (the scheme to steal the food and the pretense that she just couldn't get enough of these fascinating people) for over five hours. As Russon put it, she "simulated innocent behavior, and covertly advanced ulterior motives." Russon claims she satisfied the criterion for marking the different representations by exaggerating her niceness in the pretense and inhibiting behaviors that would give away her darker designs in the real script.

Russon offers other examples that display aspects of complex pretending. One intriguing case involved two orangutans in the Sungai Wain Forest. After a nine-year-old male named Aming was reintroduced to the preserve, the resident dominant male, Panjul, made several attempts to approach the newcomer. Each time Aming would retreat. Then Panjul tried something different. He would approach, but instead of touching Aming he would turn and begin eating leaves. This seemed to reassure Aming, who started munching on liana before becoming spooked and heading up a tree.

Russon thinks that the eating established a "conversation" of sorts. As she observed, Panjul tried several more approaches. He would eat termites, while Aming assumed a submissive posture and started eating pith from a Licuala palm. Russon found this noteworthy because no one had previously observed an orangutan in Sungai Wain eating pith from this particular palm. Eventually Aming got spooked again and retreated, and then Panjul started eating the leftover Licuala pith. Eventually, the barriers broke down and Aming mustered the confidence to stay his ground when approached by Panjul.

What do I make of this? My immediate reaction was that the two orangutans were engaged in a ritual of establishing trust that we see today in human cultures. This is particularly evident in broadly shared rituals of hospitality where guests are served a meal, a gesture of generosity on the part of the host, who is dishonored only at great peril.

Russon is more interested in the complex structure of this interaction. She argues that in these and other cases observed, the ritual eating constituted a pretense that allowed Panjul to reassure Aming that his approaches were friendly. Lest there be any doubt, Panjul's eating of pith—considered inedible by Sungai Wain orangutans—passed a clear message that the eating was a symbolic act intended to convey Panjul's benign intentions. Observers such as George Schaller have noticed similar behavior with mountain gorillas, and Russon notes that this mutual feigned interest in a common object (or activity) is a device used by chimpanzees during conflict resolution. In *The Parrot's Lament* I cited examples of such collective lies as a means of deflecting potential conflicts. Frans de Waal has argued that this kabuki dance of one party deceiving and the other acting as if deceived can bring adversaries together.

Hearing this story I could not help but think about the conversational dance that took place as Panjul and Aming pretended to eat increasingly implausible items. It seems as though they were finding a common vocabulary to pass along a message that had nothing to do with eating. This is very similar to the ways in which relationships are established and terms defined when people meet. Perhaps when we look at these eating rituals by which orangutans seem to establish benign intent we are looking at one of the origins of symbolic representation. It is not too much to imagine that at some point the ritual of eating symbolic foods such as pith from the Licuala palm might be supplanted by the gestures involved when eating such foods.

At the Dallas Zoo, I learned of some other examples of deception. Chloe, a young female chimp, often finds herself strategizing to deal with Casey, a much younger male. According to Bonnie Hendrickson, Casey can be a pest. Sometimes to distract Casey, Chloe will lead him over to something interesting like a branch or a toy and then, once he is engaged, sneak away, "ditching the younger brother," as Bonnie puts it.

Chloe's gambits get more elaborate when it comes to food. One of the ways in which keepers deliver treats to the chimp colony is to throw food from the roof of the building and cage complex that anchor one end of the large fenced enclosure. Competitive as all get out where food is concerned, Casey will run ahead as soon as Chloe starts in one direction. Rather than get in a foot race with her pesky little brother, Chloe will make eye contact with the keeper throwing the food, and then start off in one direction. As soon as Casey gets ahead of her, Chloe will plant a foot and run off in another direction, as though she were a wide receiver in football losing a defender on a down-and-out pattern. The keepers, clued in by Chloe to the game, can then toss her some food without the risk of having it stolen by her little brother.

Trading is another category of behavior that seems to reveal the way animals think. Chloe, for instance, will collect stray items for the keepers in return for treats. This could be looked at as cooperation, but it also could be characterized as trading. Gorillas, orangutans and chimps are inveterate traders, and typically they realize that there is more value to be obtained if they return an object from their cage piece by piece rather than all at once.

It turns out that many other animals have discovered that it is more profitable to sell retail than wholesale. Spock, a dolphin at Marine World, approached the head trainers, Jim Mullen, with a piece of paper and was promptly given a treat. Then he kept showing up with pieces of paper, which he would exchange for treats. In essence Spock had discovered the use of paper money. Eventually, the keepers discovered his cache of paper when they found a sheaf of papers wedged against an outflow pipe. Was Spock purposefully doling out his money sparingly, or was it that he could only retrieve the paper one sheet at a time given its inaccessible location?

The medium of exchange tends to vary with animals' tastes. Orangutans like fruit or monkey biscuits, dolphins like fish, and elephants like sweet grasses. At least that's the experience of one keeper at the International Wildlife Park in Nebraska. An elephant there got hold of a lock and established the price in alfalfa.

Some keepers have mixed feelings about trading treats for work. Once the animals run out of refuse and toys to bring to their keepers, some will resort to drastic actions. Dolphins have been known to try to take apart their tank in their search for tradable goods.

At the New York Aquarium, the keepers have trained the otters to fetch objects in return for treats. According to keeper JoAnne Basinger, Spanky has become a keen student of human expressions in his search for clues as to the value of the objects he is retrieving. She says the otter will behave differently if "we go out with an air of desperation," recalling one instance in which Spanky was loath to part with an expensive pair of sunglasses a keeper wanted very badly to get back.

The otters are not above a little cheating when it comes to dealing with humans. When treats are handed out Spanky will hide what he has been given in a loose flap of skin underneath his armpit that otters sometimes use as a place to cache favorite objects. Then he will approach JoAnne with both paws out, pretending he has not received anything yet. If given a food he doesn't like, such as squid, Spanky will go off and spit it out somewhere out of sight and then return with his hands out.

Elephants don't have such pouches, but Debbie Olson of the Indianapolis Zoo notes that they will try to conceal objects from keepers. Occasionally she will notice one of her elephants with an odd expression on its face. That's a tip-off that they have stolen food. She says that they will quickly shove the food into their mouths and then screw up their lips so that the keepers can't see what they have concealed.

Olson notes that elephants are fundamentally honest, and while they will resort to deception, their hearts are often not in it. Harry Peachey of the Columbus Zoo agrees, although he recalls one deft example of pickpocketing staged by Koko in 1978. Peachey typically carried a ballpoint pen in the pocket of his shirt. One time while he was in the elephant enclosure with Koko, the elephant kept taking the pen out of Peachey's breast pocket. He would give it back to the keeper when asked, but Harry grew tired of the interruptions caused by the repeated thefts, and shifted the pen to his pants pocket.

He resumed his chores and forgot about the pen until he left the enclosure and heard a clink. Looking back, he saw the pen on the floor of Koko's stall. Peachey surmises that Koko had somehow snaked his trunk into the keeper's pants pocket and lifted the pen. The keeper was impressed that Koko maintained the deception until he had left the stall.

Like some dolphin keepers, Peachey does not encourage trade and barter with the elephants. This is for practical reasons, since the combination of their strength, the dexterity of their trunks, and their natural inquisitiveness means that they can get ahold of almost anything if they put their minds to it. "Usually, if they get something, we just ask for it back," says Peachey. At some point later he will give them a treat or encouragement. "If I'd had to barter for that pen," he notes, "I would be bartering for everything from that point onwards."

Escape is another category in which animals can display glorious ingenuity. Fu Manchu's escape was a masterpiece of deception, patience, and engineering. Many animals, however, like to get out now and then, and apart from the octopus, there are a number of other surprisingly gifted escape artists. One of the most tantalizing stories arrived in a letter from Eleanor

Marvel, a woman who grew up in the Midwest and who re-
called a series of extraordinary incidents from childhood visits
to her grandparents' farm in Ashland, Wisconsin.

Ms. Marvel and her sisters would travel to Ashland in August in the 1920s and 30s during her father's annual vacation
from his duties as director of religious education at a big
church in the Chicago area. As she notes, during that period,
farmers were still making the transition from horse-drawn machinery to tractors, and her grandparents, being quite old,
were perfectly content to stay with horses. The horses included
a spirited mare named Dolly, who was part Arabian, and the
old farmers would regularly let the horses, the bull, and the
cows go off together to graze. As Ms. Marvel notes, the bull
would regularly come in with the horses before the cows returned for their evening milking.

As she recalls the incident, one summer afternoon they
found Dolly and the bull loose in the yard around the farmhouse. They should have been in the barnyard, safely secured
behind a wooden gate that was latched by a long iron hook
that would go into an eye hook on an adjoining fence post. The
weight of the gate kept the hook in place. The girls all swore
that none of them had left the gate open. The incident was for-
gotten until two days later. Once again they found Dolly and
the bull loose in the yard. Again the girls protested their inno-
cence. To find out what was going on, Eleanor's father assigned one of her sisters the role of sentry, installing her in a
window of the farmhouse that looked out on the barnyard.

This time there was a witness when the bull and horses arrived in the afternoon. After a while inside the barnyard, the
bull wandered over to the gate with Dolly close behind him.
Hooking his horns under the gate, the bull lifted it a few
inches, releasing the tension on the hook. Dolly then undid the
hook by lifting it with her nose. When the bull let the gate fall

from his horns, the gate fell open enough for the two pals to squeeze through in search of greener grass.

Ms. Marvel modestly ended her enchanting account by asking whether this was an example of animal intelligence or an accident. I have no idea. It involves a boggling combination of abilities, including cooperation and coordination of movements by two different species. If orangutans or gorillas did this, there is no question that we would be inclined to credit this to cleverness. But a horse and a bull? I can't verify this story from long, long ago, but I can't resist retelling it either. I'm also grateful to Ms. Marvel for her beguiling glimpse into the farm life of a simpler time.

Chapter Nine

CHIMP SOLACE AND SHARING AMONG THE VAMPIRES

Empathy and Cooperation

Empathy is as human as cruelty. Both require the capacity to be aware of the feelings of others. But empathy goes beyond awareness to an ability to share the feelings of others. More than understanding that others have thoughts and feelings, it requires an ability to feel the suffering of others. Perhaps the best side of humanity comes out in times of crisis when people feel the suffering of others, and then bring their intelligence to bear to alleviate that suffering. It involves intangibles like mind reading and emotional intelligence, but also caring for those beyond the immediate family. Mothers of many species will risk or even sacrifice their lives to protect their young, but this devotion can be seen as a selfish legacy, an attempt to ensure the perpetuation of the mother's genes. Empathy, on the other hand, can work at cross-purposes to genetic commandments, since gestures of empathy in no way enhance one's prospects for reproduction, getting food, or solidifying one's role in the social order. Quite often they involve sacrifice, or at least the expenditure of energy.

This is why the notion of animal empathy is as controversial for biologists as animal intelligence is for behavioral scientists. When I asked marine biologist Richard Connor about marine mammal empathy, he joked, "Kindness—no biologist has seen it." He notes that while much has been made about dolphins rescuing drowning humans (including the celebrated Cuban shipwrecked child Elian Gonzalez, who claims that when he began slipping off the piece of wreckage to which he was clinging, dolphins pushed him back on), the more cynical scientists say that you don't hear about the seamen who were pushed out to sea instead of in toward the shore. Connor is not in that camp, having written articles about animals' ability to form bonds across taxonomic divisions.

If, as Connor jokes, no biologist has seen kindness, neither have many psychologists. In *Wild Minds*, Marc Hauser cites a number of experiments (done in times less sensitive to animal rights) in which various scientists discovered that rats seemed to choose not to eat if their getting food caused suffering for fellow rats, and other work in which rhesus monkeys chose to deny themselves food rather than cause injury to other rhesus monkeys. As always there are alternative explanations—e.g. the rats might have been avoiding unpleasant noises, including the squealing of fellow rats—and Hauser argues that the work does not prove the capacity for empathy. His feeling is that animals are not capable of empathy nor of shame, sympathy, guilt, or loyalty, because they lack self-awareness. He leaves the door open for future work that might show this capacity in other creatures, but for now he argues that there is no evidence for a sense of self in animals that would permit empathy, which for Hauser "represents an emotional fusion of self and other."

That is the scientifically conservative case thoughtfully articulated but, as Hauser admits, lack of evidence is not proof that something does not exist. Applying these standards of proof to human examples of empathy might lead us to conclude that it does not exist in our species either. Christopher Hitchens once published the argument that Mother Teresa, a Nobel Peace Prize–winning embodiment of empathy, was nothing more than a calculating and self-serving publicity hound.

It is true that much of what we perceive as kindness and loyalty in the animal kingdom can be described (accurately or not) as reward-driven behavior or the desire of a social animal to protect its meal ticket and extended family. Books have been written about how dogs have made suckers of humans, and how dolphins treat each other abysmally in the wild. But then there are stories that are not so easily reduced.

Distinguished marine biologist Ken Norris cited one case of mutual aid in whale society that seemed to involve awareness as well as empathy. The interpretation hinged on the unusual behavior of a group of pilot whales after one of their numbers was harpooned. Two other pilot whales held it up as it was dragged back toward the whaling boat. As they got close to the boat, however, the companion whales pushed their wounded comrade down and away from the boat, contrary to the per-ceived preprogrammed behavior of keeping a distressed whale on the surface where it can breathe. Norris suggests that the companion whales realized that it was more important to keep the wounded pilot whale out of the whaling boat than to keep it on the surface at that point. And if they realized this, they also realized that they were putting themselves at risk by approach-ing the whaling boat.

Tragedy, both human and animal, brought out a striking in-stance of what appeared to be kindness in the chimp colony at the Dallas Zoo in Texas. The chimps in Dallas have a large, new outdoor enclosure with standing and fallen trees, as well as brushy areas where they can retreat if they want to get out of the spotlight. The chimps have a well-organized hierarchy and they have also worked out a cooperative system with the human keepers.

Toby is the alpha male. Now about forty-five, he was caught in the wild and spent the first eight years of his life in a medical laboratory. He spent his first twenty years at the Dallas Zoo in isolation. He began to live with other chimps in 1990, and despite the trials of his life has turned out to be a model parent and leader. Valerie Beardsley, a keeper who has been working with the chimp colony for eight years, says, for instance, that Toby will usher all the other chimps into their night cages at the end of the day, as though to make sure they are safe before coming in himself.

Beardsley lost her daughter a few years back, and when she returned to work, some of the chimps seemed to sense that she was sad, although she did her best not to let her feelings affect her relations with them. During this period, Beardsley says that Victoria, a low-ranking female, would come up to her and give a reassuring *"oh oh oh"* sound with a concerned look on her face. She would also come up and sit quietly with Beardsley, who was profoundly moved by these expressions of comfort and sympathy coming from another species.

Toby suffered his own loss. Beardsley believes that it testifies to his noble character that apart from expressing his own grief, he took it upon himself to buck up the humans who were equally upset by a tragic accident. The incident involved an escape that led to the death of Judy, an eleven-year-old female.

Judy had come from the Tulsa Zoo, and by the account of keeper Bonnie Hendrickson, she was an extraordinary chimp. "When she came here, she did all the right things," says Hendrickson. "She knew who to submit to and who to bully." According to the keepers, Toby absolutely adored Judy. When she was threatened, she knew she could run to Toby and he would put his arms around her and protect her.

Still, she might have missed her former home. One day, she got up in the swaying branches of a tree and swung herself across a huge gap to get to the top of the high fence around the enclosure. The leap she made had been deemed impossible by the zoo designers. At first she strolled through the zebra enclosure, taking the time to politely greet one of the zebras by offering the female a pronated wrist. Not understanding chimp etiquette, the zebra simply sniffed and snorted.

Then she made her fatal mistake. Before alarmed zoo officials could get to her, she climbed the nearest tall piece of wood, which turned out to be a telephone pole. Touching the wrong wire, she was electrocuted and fell to the ground.

Even before she climbed the pole, her escape had caused pandemonium in the chimp colony. Toby climbed a tall pecan tree (something he almost never does) and called to her for about twenty minutes.

The next morning, he did something that convinced Hendrickson and Beardsley that Toby was trying to reassure the humans who were weeping and obviously distressed: he went out of his way to play with the keepers, something he had rarely done previously. He invented games, he clowned, he played tag with their fingers through the wire mesh that separated them. He played chase games. He would hunch up his shoulders, or use a funny play walk. Says Beardsley, "After a while, we were laughing through our tears. Toby seemed to know that we needed comforting." After forty-five minutes, Beardsley and Hendrickson felt a lot better, and Toby rejoined the other chimps.

Even if Toby hadn't seen Judy's fall, he could have sensed that she was never coming back from the behavior of the keepers. Since chimps regularly pick up English words, it is even possible that he knew that she was dead from eavesdropping on the obviously deeply distressed keepers. A reductionist might say that Toby was seeking to reinforce his bonds with the keepers after a traumatic event, and yes, that's possible. But Toby did not solicit grooming or engage in any other behaviors that chimps use to comfort themselves when anxious. Beardsley and Hendrickson felt that his actions were taken to address their needs, not his.

Cooperation is a lot easier to demonstrate. Beardsley says that Chloe, one of the females, will do chores if asked. Beardsley will say, "Chloe, get that paper," and Chloe will go off looking for something that does not belong in the enclosure and bring it back to Beardsley. This cooperation is not selfless— in her desire to find things to trade for rewards, Chloe will sometimes take things from one of the babies and offer to trade them with the keepers. Chimps are extremely conscious of social rank, and Beardsley says that Victoria, one of the lowest-ranking chimps, will pick flowers and offer them as a present to Beardsley, the highest ranking female in Victoria's eyes.

At the Indianapolis Zoo, an elephant provided physical if not emotional help for keeper Debbie Olson. One of the keepers' chores is to clean the elephant yard. To carry away manure, they use large carts. One day, a manure cart was down in a park area of the elephant enclosure below the yard Olson was cleaning. Olson found that she didn't have the strength to pull the cart up the hill to the yard by herself.

As she struggled, Debbie began thinking about whom she could ask for help with the cart, although she did not say anything out loud. One of the female elephants, named Sophie, had been watching Debbie struggle, and suddenly she walked over and pushed the cart up the hill. Olson says that the elephant had never received any training to do chores.

If there may be more empathy at work in the behavior of animals than most scientists are willing to acknowledge, there may also be less empathy and kindness in human daily life than we would like to believe. In the ordinary course of life, humanity's selfish instincts are more often tempered by fear of punishment than by adherence to some abstract moral code. Indeed, in many tribal and some modern societies, moral imperatives are not general, as in "love thy neighbor" or "thou shalt not kill," but quite specific as in "thou shalt not covet thy immediate neighbor's wife, but stealing a woman from the next village is fine," or "thou shalt not cut that particular tree or your crops will fail and your wife will become barren" (both of these examples come from New Guinea). Rather than a general moral sense, most people have a more flexible and pragmatic approach, e.g. apologizing insincerely for something to get someone off your back.

Lying in bed one morning, I encountered a hilarious example of this in my two young children. At the time, Alec was three and Sofia was four. I was abruptly roused from sleep as I heard Sofia thundering down the hallway past our bedroom with Alec in hot pursuit, howling as he ran after his sister. The stampede was accompanied by an audio Doppler effect, with the howls rising in volume as he approached the door, and then decreasing as he continued down the hallway.

Sofia is pretty fast, so she could stay ahead of her little brother. When she got to the end of the hallway, she nimbly reversed course and ran back the other way with Alec's howls once again rising and then falling as they passed the door. Clearly she had taken something that Alec thought was rightfully his, and so as she passed a third time I said sternly, "Sofia, what did you do?"

Coming back the other way, she shouted as she ran past the door, "I said I was sorry," and then as she passed again, "and it was an accident!" Despite our efforts to impart notions of right and wrong to Sofia's four-year-old brain, she clearly thought that these phrases had magic power to justify her wrongdoing, whether or not the words were uttered as the result of any genuine feeling of remorse. In functional terms, how different was Sofia's repentance than seeking absolution during confession in a church?

Alec is not above this kind of pragmatic morality himself. Just before his fourth birthday, our babysitter, Lera, brought Alec over to her boyfriend's house (Alec worships Seth because he owns a serious-looking truck). Seth asked Alec whether he had been a good boy and whether Santa had come down the chimney and given him a present. According to Lera, Alec replied, "I was a very bad boy this year, but I tricked Santa and he gave me presents!"

Another issue worth considering is whether behavior can be considered empathetic or selfless if it is encoded in the genes. One of the most compelling testaments to the human desire to help one another happens when people volunteer to give blood during times of crisis. In the aftermath of the September 11 attacks on the World Trade Center, so many people volunteered to donate blood that the flow temporarily overwhelmed the Red Cross's capacity to receive and store the life-sustaining fluid. As it happens, humans are not the only animal to share blood willingly with fellow members of the species.

Perhaps the most notable blood sharers are animals that have inspired fear and loathing for centuries: vampire bats. In the case of the bats, they are not replenishing blood lost through injury, but helping each other out with food when a fellow bat has a temporary liquidity crisis. Vampire bats in Costa Rica have done nothing less than develop a blood-banking system in which they will take in more blood than they need when feeding, and then regurgitate some when called upon by a needy colleague.

The vampire blood exchange, first described by biologist Gerald Wilkinson in 1983, caught the attention of economists because it represents perhaps the optimum solution to a problem called the "Prisoner's Dilemma" that has bedeviled game theorists since it was first proposed by the great mathematician John von Neumann over fifty years ago. The game poses a situation in which a prisoner who sells out his accomplice stands to benefit from leniency, unless his accomplice separately sells him out as well. The third option is that neither sells the other out, and each serves a sentence longer than if he sold the other out, but shorter than if they were both sold out. The game is interesting because it offers a way to explore whether cooperation is logical as well as virtuous for both animals and humans.

What's the best thing to do? Robert Axelrod, a political scientist at the University of Michigan, tested fourteen strategies in a variety of circumstances over a number of years and discovered that, as the game is repeated over and over, one successful strategy tends to win out. Called "tit for tat," it simply says that if someone gives you something, reciprocate; if they don't, reciprocate selfishness with selfishness.

The key to this system is the fact that the player is likely to encounter other players again, what Axelrod calls "the shadow of the future." If this is not true, there is every incentive to cheat— to drink, but not share, blood. Thus the larger and more anonymous the situation, the greater the incentive to be selfish. This works in human societies, but it also applies to animal groups, where nature has had the luxury to work out the optimum response to the Prisoner's Dilemma through countless experiments over the millennia.

The collapse of stock prices has given this game theory problem some topicality, because actions by brokerage houses in the spring of 2000 offered a case study that contrasts dramatically to the solution derived by bats. As the markets cratered that spring, a number of overextended investors faced margin calls in which brokerage houses demanded that they contribute more collateral in accounts where they had borrowed money from brokerage houses, or face the prospect of having the broker sell their holdings at distressed prices. Clearly this is not in the broker's long-term interest, since these sales only increase the downward pressure on share prices, prompting more margin calls and further panic. But this is exactly what they did.

The difference between vampire bats and brokers is not that one is a blood-sucking rodent and the other, well . . . No, the difference may be the simple notion that the more anonymous the situation is, the easier it is to be selfish. There is no larger or more anonymous forum than the markets for stocks. This is by design; free markets are predicated on the notion that the greater good for all will come from many individuals who have the opportunity to act on their immediate self-interest. That may be, but when seas get rough, there is little to stop investors from sinking the lifeboats in their zeal to be the first to abandon ship. Robert Shiller, the Yale economist whose book *Irrational Exuberance* explores the perils of the present market, once devised a survey to probe whether investors felt any responsibility to the overall system. When asked whether they might reduce selling in a crash out of a sense of social responsibility, only eight percent of 123 institutional investors responded positively in a typical sample. With twenty-five percent responding yes, individual investors showed slightly more civic consciousness—or naiveté. We would likely be better off if we turned to vampire bats to design our equities markets.

The bats probably don't know that they are community-minded, or that they have worked out a solution to a problem in game theory that bedeviled a generation of the world's best economists. The bats are probably unaware that their loathsome reputation camouflages a system of sharing that humanity has tried and failed to emulate. But perhaps the most beguiling aspect of the genius of evolution is that its ingenuity is in the eye of the beholder.

Finally, a word about moral sense and good behavior. When a mother cat suffers grievous burns as she returns again and again to a burning building to save her kittens, we attribute this to a powerful maternal instinct rather than a moral decision. When those brave souls of September 11 sacrificed their lives by staying behind in the towers of the World Trade Center to help others escape, we applaud these heroic acts as conscious choices. They probably were; every now and then in war and times of crisis, people will knowingly put aside concerns for their own safety to help others. These soaring moments of sacrifice become enshrined as a moral beacon for humanity.

Chapter Ten

THE STARLING THAT CHARMED MOZART

Animal Arts and Sciences

It is relatively easy to understand the thinking that goes into tool use or toolmaking. It is somewhat harder to decode other behaviors where an animal might make seemingly intelligent use of its environment, but it is unclear whether the behavior is the result of individual experience, learning from others, or a genetic predisposition. Self-medication falls into this category. So many animals use plants and soils to medicate themselves that an entire field called zoopharmacognosy has arisen to study the phenomenon. Still, it is unclear what it all means.

Here is a case where the overlap between human and animal extends to the point of using the same natural substance to treat the same problem. Holly Dublin of the World Wildlife Fund discovered that both elephants and Kenyan natives use the leaves of a particular tree from the Boraginaceae family to induce labor. Michael Huffman of the University of Kyoto noticed that women from the WaTongwe tribe in Tanzania and chimpanzees in the Mahale Mountains both eat the leaves of *Vernonia Amygdalina* when they suffer from intestinal ailments. Around the world, people will eat charcoal to settle stomach complaints. So do red colobus monkeys on the island of Zanzibar, who eat mangoes and almonds with a high concentration of toxic phenols that are absorbed by charcoal, according to studies done by David Cooney of the University of Wyoming and Thomas Struhsaker of Duke University.

Some animals value natural medicines sufficiently to pass them around. John Robinson, a primatologist and director of research at the Wildlife Conservation Society in New York City, noticed odd behavior by wedge-capped capuchin monkeys (*Cebus olivaceus*) while in Venezuela more than two decades ago. When they found a millipede, they would rub it all over their bodies and then often pass it on to another capuchin who would do the same. Sometimes three or four monkeys would share the same bug, and then they would rub against each other. Subsequently, Ximena Valderrama, a Columbia University anthropologist, collected the millipedes as part of a study and sent them to Cornell University, where they were analyzed by the renowned entomologist Thomas Eisner and his colleague Athula Attygalle. Analysis of the secretions revealed that they contained powerful insecticides and disinfectants called benzoquinones. Valderrama found it telling that the animals only used the millipedes during the rainy season when they are vulnerable to botfly—one of the tropics' most intrusive pests. Botflies lay their larvae under a mammal's skin where they grow into large lumps before emerging to make life miserable for other unfortunates.

We should not be surprised that a wide range of animals has found ways to treat ailments. In zoos, the regularity with which animals turn to humans when they or their offspring are hurt or sick suggests that animals know that they need help when they are ill, and know where to turn to seek it. Harry Peachey of the Columbus Zoo believes that experience with self-medication in the wild accounts for the extraordinary cooperation of the elephants he cares for when they need medical care. Belinda, for instance, developed an infection on the side of her face. Without using any restraints, veterinarians were able to lance and irrigate the infection to drain away the pus. Belinda calmly cooperated despite the fact that the procedure involved cutting her skin. "It probably made her feel better," recalls Peachey, "and they seem to understand that we are trying to help them get well." He says that elephants will actually position themselves so that human doctors have better access to an injury or affliction.

At Wanarisit in Borneo, the orangutans being rehabilitated will allow human doctors to put a splint on broken bones even while they are conscious, a painful process that would test the resolve of a human patient in a doctor's office, much less a wild animal in the care of another species. Veteran animal trainer Tim Desmond recalls that at Marineland of the Pacific, when a sick infant killer whale slipped to the bottom of its tank some years ago, the first thing its alarmed and inexperienced orca parents did was to lift their heads out of the water and look to the keepers, as though saying, "What do we do now?"

So much for the body. A sentient creature must feed the soul, too, and a number of animals have also pursued the arts. Paintings done by chimps and elephants, for instance, are often sold to zoo patrons during fund-raising drives. Most of these works are purchased for their novelty value, but some keepers insist that you can see in some animal artwork the glimmer ings of a individual trying to express itself.

Ruby, an Asian elephant at the Phoenix Zoo, was one such budding expressionist. Before she died during an operation at age twenty-seven, she loved nothing better than to put brush to canvas. Anita Schanberger, now curator of mammals at the Dallas Zoo, worked with Ruby at Phoenix. She recalls that often Ruby would be eavesdropping with an eye to her window when the keepers talked about her. If they discussed whether they should have Ruby paint, she would get all excited when she heard the word "paint."

Her favorite colors were red, yellow, blue, and green. Because they knew her preferences, the keepers paid attention when she varied her palette. One time a man had a heart attack outside her enclosure. Ruby paid close attention when a fire truck rumbled up with lights flashing. The truck and its lights were red, yellow and white. Later that day, when Ruby had a chance to paint, she chose these colors for her work. She also showed a preference for painting the colors that people were wearing. If a keeper was wearing blue, for instance, she would draw blue.

Art is intensely personal, and we might expect paintings to vary with the artist and perhaps reflect his or her personality. Debbie Olson notes that one of the elephants, named Ivory, uses very aggressive strokes. She says that Ivory's paintings are much more harsh than the more free-form works of other elephants.

An appreciation of art and music go together (in humans both abilities tend to be associated with the right hemisphere of the brain). In Thailand, at the Thai Elephant Conservation Center, a former logging camp that has become something of a tourist attraction, a number of the residents have taken to playing musical instruments proffered by David Lair, an expatriate American and David Sulzer, a Columbia University neurologist and composer. As reported by Eric Scigliano in the *New York Times*, the humans merely presented the elephants with traditional Thai instruments such as slit drums and gongs as well as harmonicas and thundersheets, showed them how to make sounds, and then taught them to start and stop on cue. The humans have recorded the sounds and produced a CD. According to Scigliano, Lair has proposed a type of Turing test to determine whether the results are music: Play the CD without divulging the identity of the performers and ask a group of sophisticated listeners what it is. My sense is that given the highly abstract nature of some modern music, the risk of embarrassment in this proposed test would fall more on the humans than the elephants.

According to Scigliano, one interesting tidbit turned up by this venture was the suggestion that elephants have a sense of dissonance. When Sulzer introduced an off-key note into the keyboard of the xylophone, a seven-year-old female named Prathida at first avoided playing the note, until one day she started playing it and wouldn't stop. She seemed to recognize that it was special.

Another natural musician is the much-maligned starling. The starling came to the United States in 1890 when a drug manufacturer named Eugene Schieffelin released sixty in Central Park as part of his plan to introduce to the Americas all the birds mentioned in Shakespeare. As with the introduction of most exotic species it proved to be a disaster (poison ivy, for instance, was brought from the US to England as a decorative plant), and in the case of the starling it was a memorable disaster—and we are still living with the consequences. Ted Gup commemorated their one hundredth anniversary in the US by ticking off their impact in an Op-Ed piece in the *New York Times*. Now numbering in the hundreds of millions in the US starlings spread diseases such as histoplasmosis and toxoplasmosis among humans, and carry Newcastle disease to chickens; they have brought about airplane crashes, eaten through whole crops of potatoes, and crowded out native species.

On the other hand, they can sing. The good side of the starling was offered in an article in the *American Scientist*, also published during the bird's centennial year. Many songbirds have nice songs, but starlings are also gifted mimics whose vocalizations have attracted admirers such as Mozart and Schubert as well as the bard of Avon. In the *American Scientist* article, psychologists Meredith West and Andrew King discussed how a pet starling's song may have been immortalized by Mozart in the context of the bird's extraordinary gifts for vocal mimicry. With painstaking musicology and historical research coupled with their own experiments, West and King reconstruct interactions between Mozart and a starling he bought as a pet, in which each seemed to influence the other.

As West and King note, starlings are capable of a wide range of sounds ranging from whistles and screeches to clicks and rattles. They copy the sounds they hear around them, possibly using their vocal mimicry to probe for responses in those around them. If reactions are what they want, they must be very pleased with what they get from humans when they say, "Does Hammacher Schlemmer have a toll-free number?" or chant "Defense!" when the television is on (something this particular starling might have picked up from watching a basketball game).

Sometimes the utterances are appropriate to the occasion, according to West and King, and sometimes they are not. They report that one bird kept shouting, "Basic research!" as he struggled with a string wrapped around his head. More understandably, another kept screeching the words, "I have a question" while she was held as her feet were being treated for an infection. Still another bird, raised by a Japanese family, used the Japanese word *mizu*, which means water, whenever she alighted on a faucet. More to the point of the Mozart mystery, West and King's research showed that starlings might repeat a phrase such as "Does Hammacher Schlemmer have a toll-free number?" after just one hearing. This is important.

On May 27, 1784, Mozart noted in his diary the purchase of a starling from a pet shop, and he also jotted down the transcription of a melody sung by the bird. The melody, according to West and King, was very similar to a theme in the last movement of Mozart's Piano Concerto in G Major, K. 453, which, the authors note, was not played in public for another two weeks. Given their research on the bird's abilities, they surmise that

Mozart might have visited the shop prior to buying the bird, and might have hummed or whistled the melody absently as he strolled around.

Some biographers have argued that Mozart actually borrowed the theme from the starling and incorporated it into his concerto, but King and West argue that this is unlikely since the composer completed the concerto six weeks before he purchased the bird. On the other hand, they argue that a later short piece by Mozart, "A Musical Joke," reveals many characteristics of starling mimicry that would have been apparent to a person with as gifted an ear as Mozart. Starlings will piece together odd fragments like the *William Tell Overture* and "Rockabye Baby," and will repeat a theme, slightly changing it to add off-key notes. As West and King note: "The presence of drawn-out, wandering phrases of uncertain structure also is characteristic of starling soliloquies. Finally, the abrupt end, as if the instruments had simply ceased to work, has the signature of starlings written all over it." The Mozart work, written sporadically over a three-year period, was completed eight days after the starling's death, and West and King speculate that it was "an appropriate musical farewell, a requiem of sorts for his avian friend."

At the beginning of this chapter I urged readers to put aside worries about whether any of these stories of overlap between animal and human abilities imply higher mental abilities. Let's now let the spoilsports back into the room. Yes, the fact that a starling can whistle Mozart, or even inspire Mozart, does not make the composer's pet a musical peer.

Birds that learn their song mimic for various reasons. During periods of rapid evolutionary change, for instance, when many birds are vocalizing within earshot of each other, some scientists argue that songbirds that are adapted to a particular niche might gain some genetic advantage by having offspring that can pick out the subtle differences of their parents' song from among similar songs of others in the species. Mimicry might also enable a bird to convince other birds to feed it. The bird may have a near-perfect memory for melody and what seems to be a creative and mischievous talent for improvisation, but it may simply be employing a starling rule: "Listen to the sounds made by your parents and then slightly alter them to provide a song for your own chicks." But then again, maybe it has a sense of fun as it follows this rule.

Chapter Eleven

LOST CATS AND QUANTUM MECHANICS

Language and Communication

Having written a great deal over the years about the question of whether animals can understand and use language, I have greatly enjoyed the opportunity to get away from this issue and explore other higher mental abilities. Stories about trade and barter, tool use, and deception draw on various aspects of intelligence, some related to communication and some not. It is hard, however, to ignore the language issue entirely.

For one thing, one of the most suggestive indicators that there is a mind behind a particular behavior is an unambiguous, novel, and clear message of intent that lies outside an animal's normal behavioral repertoire. Recall the female octopus's rejection of a slightly spoiled shrimp. Holding Jean Baul's gaze while she shoved the shrimp down the drain suggested to Jean that the octopus was sending a message, while the action of stuffing the bad shrimp down the drain seemed to convey a very clear message about the quality of the food in the establishment in which the octopus found itself a guest. Because the animal was an octopus (a solitary mollusk that has little social interaction with its own kind), it is a stretch to suggest that the animal was intentionally signaling to Jean. It's possible, however, that the octopus was doing exactly what it seemed to be doing, in which case the little female octopus was offering us a view of a whole new world. Moreover, there are a host of similar stories involving far less controversial animals.

Diana Reiss has been studying dolphin cognition and anatomy for nearly twenty years. She did her Ph.D. at Temple University based on research she did in France in 1981 at the CNRZ, France's National Center for Zoological Research, which is a rough equivalent of the US National Science Foundation. Her dissertation was on bioacoustics, and her experimental subject was a female dolphin kept in an eighty-foot-wide tank. As part of her work, she trained the young female, named Circe, to eat parts of fish that Reiss would cut up into heads, middle sections, and tails. The young female readily ate the heads and middles, but spat out the tails. This precipitated a series of incidents, and then a study that gave Reiss some insight into the mental powers of the dolphin.

Reiss used straightforward operant conditioning techniques to train the dolphin to eat the various sections of the fish. This meant that she would reward the dolphin when it went to its station in front of her, and if the dolphin acted up, Reiss would step back ten or fifteen feet, in essence enforcing a "time-out" as a mother might do with an obstreperous child. After the dolphin spat out the fish tails a few times, Reiss noticed that Circe would eat the tails if the fins were cut off. She began cutting off the fins, wryly noting to herself that the dolphin was training her rather than vice versa. Occasionally she would slip up, however, and give the dolphin a tail with the fins still on. This did not pass unnoticed.

The female would spit out the offending morsel, of course, but then swim back to the other side of the tank and remain there positioned vertically in the water. Circe would wait there for a short time and then return to her station. The first time the female did this, Reiss was amused. But when she slipped up again, and the dolphin again retreated to the other side of the tank, Reiss realized that the animal was giving Reiss a time-out just as she did when the dolphin did something wrong.

Reiss decided on the spot to try an experiment. She started deliberately putting tails with fins into the mix of fish that she gave to Circe. Sure enough, every time she did this, the dolphin would give her a time-out. It became perfectly clear that the animal had appropriated Reiss's own signaling system for her own purposes.

Reiss argues that this exchange between her and the dolphin was what communication is all about. Specifically, the dolphin used terms (in this case movements) whose meaning was mutually agreed upon to make her feelings known to Reiss. For Reiss, this synchronizing of patterns is the essence of communication. Moreover, she notes that an observer watching the two would have no idea how to interpret what was going on. Reiss understood perfectly, however, because she recognized the dolphin's use of a rule that she herself had established.

There is, however, one group of outsiders for whom this exchange would have made perfect sense. In the late 1980s and early 1990s I interviewed a number of scientists at Palo Alto's Institute for Research on Learning who were working on the question of what goes on in a conversation. Their purpose was completely practical: They wanted to develop software systems that can respond to and interpret everyday speech.

The quest was part of a general endeavor in computers to create artificial intelligence, the name given to attempts to replicate human cognitive abilities in software. This lofty ambition has been thwarted by the same ambiguities and unresolved questions that have dogged the comparison of animal and human cognitive abilities. It is difficult to model something if there is no agreed-upon definition of what it is, and that certainly is the case with both intelligence and language. Those who study intelligence are still divided as to whether we have one intelligence that is the product of several abilities, or several intelligences, each of which is supported by different parts of the brain and different wiring between those parts. There is no question that damage to specific parts of the brain impairs specific cognitive abilities, but it is also true that in the very young and in certain other cases the brain finds a way to work around certain types of damage. One of the most startling examples of this involves people born without hands who develop fine motor control over their feet and toes.

With regard to the study of language, linguistics remains without a consensus on the deep structure of language. Then there is another debate about whether language derives from one particular set of genes isolated from other higher mental abilities, or whether it derives from the programming of an assortment of mental abilities. There are many other points of dispute as well, such as whether human thought is possible at all without language.

All these points of dispute amount to an enormous headache if you are trying to design a thinking machine. Those who based language comprehension software on Noam Chomsky's ideas of an underlying grammar got nowhere, but those who tried other models did not do much better. So some of the bright folks at the IRL abandoned ideology and various theories of language and began looking at what happens during a conversation.

Out of this exercise came the notion that much of conversation involves defining the terms of conversation. This includes coming to a mutual understanding of the relationship between the two speakers, and from there what the conversation will be about—in essence, establishing the context that allows two speakers to understand the various shades of meaning of the messages passed back and forth. The phrase "I'm not happy with these results" has one meaning if George Costanza of *Seinfeld* mutters the remark, and quite another if the speaker is a murderous Mafia boss talking to an underling.

Much of the communication between humans involves nonlinguistic factors, such as facial expression, tone of voice, eye movements, body language, pauses, etc. More interesting, however, is the notion that the very meaning of words remains in some indefinite state until these terms of reference have been established.

I like this notion of meaning. It did not fit into the research I was doing when I visited IRL, but it stayed with me. Subsequently, IRL lost its funding from struggling Xerox Corporation, and then was merged into WestED, a large educational research, development, and service agency. Many of IRL's researchers have since gone on to other work, and work on this simple but compelling idea of how meanings are assigned seems to have petered out.

Still, the idea that meanings remain in something akin to a quantum haze until grounded in a specific conversation has great salience today. It also accords with a relatively new school of physics that sees laws as emergent rather than immutable and universal. Reductionists, who dominate the hard sciences, argue that all physical phenomena can be reduced to equations that describe the fundamental laws of the universe. The reductionist quest is to find those equations that reconcile presently contradictory phenomena such as the workings of the invisible quantum world and the laws that govern life in the visible world in a "grand unification." The new school of physics, developed by physicists frustrated by the complexity of many forms of matter that cannot be described in terms of the interaction of fundamental particles, argues that at its most elementary the universe is not governed by laws, but that laws emerge as systems become organized and increasingly complex. It's a notion abhorrent to particle physicists, because it eliminates the possibility of grand unification.

What is anathema to particle physicists, however, may be a bonanza for those seeking to understand the meaning of words. Perhaps a word exists before use in a type of quantum haze as potential with the possibility of an enormous number of meanings. Through conversation these meanings become more restricted and refined as the context and the speakers establish whether the conversation is friendly or formal, between peers or among speakers of different status, etc., all of which restrict the reference of the term. So if two guys are standing on the street talking about a friend and one says to the other, "That's a righteous brother," the word "righteous" takes on connotations of loyalty and courage, while the same phrase uttered by a preacher in a church would ground the word "righteous" in its religious meaning as moral and faithful. Then again, if someone walked into a music store and mentioned the Righteous Brothers, the clerk would instantly assume they were talking about a white soul band from the '60s.

Let's look at such emergent meanings in terms of Reiss's young dolphin who decided to turn the tables and train her trainer, moving backwards to the other side of the tank to mean something like, "Pay attention; you just did something wrong." This is important because the dolphin was not literally mimicking or mirroring Reiss's use of the time-out (which Reiss used when the dolphin failed to stay at her station or some other infraction of the rules), but extracting a general meaning that she turned to her own purposes. Just as in the case of conversation, the female dolphin's action seemed to be predicated on a common understanding of the meaning of a time-out.

The possibility that Circe, the young dolphin, was taking the first steps to develop a language to communicate with Reiss comes with a cascade of other implications. For one thing, if the dolphin was sending a message, it implies that the dolphin assumed that Reiss would understand the meaning of her movements as being the same as when Reiss herself stepped back. This, in turn, implies that the dolphin assumed that Reiss would understand what the dolphin was doing, meaning that the dolphin understood that Reiss would understand messages sent by the dolphin.

If so, this exchange suggests that the dolphin has a theory of mind, meaning that she is aware of another's state of knowledge. Critics might argue that the dolphin was mechanistically mimicking Reiss under the simple rule that moving back means, "No eat fish tail." But the simple rule is a more awkward fit than the possibility that the dolphin was attaching a meaning to Reiss's action and then appropriating the meaning for her own uses. It is also possible that the dolphin could extract this meaning without realizing that Reiss knew what it meant; e.g. she came to the conclusion that moving back when there is a dust-up over fish tails is a general law of the universe. Which do you think is the most likely?

Though not provable, I think it most likely that the dolphin was doing what it looked like she was doing. If so, she was also demonstrating what is called "program-level imitation." This is a sophisticated type of observational learning in which the student understands the purpose of the actions being imitated rather than blindly mimicking a series of movements.

Although Reiss's impromptu study of the dolphin's appropriation of the time-out signal got a lot of interest when she submitted her thesis for her Ph.D., she never published her dissertation. Science proceeds largely unaware of such examples. This is sad, because such impromptu behaviors can sometimes offer more insight into the mind of the animal than the study itself.

For instance, a decade later, in the course of a study of vocal mimicry with Atlantic bottlenose dolphins, Reiss came across anecdotal evidence of dolphins appropriating human words for their own purposes. This was in 1993 at Marine World Africa USA, where Reiss worked studying dolphin communication supported by the Marine World Foundation.

The study centered on teaching the dolphins to use an underwater keyboard. The board had nine squares to which Reiss could attach various white plastic symbols, which would be the "words" the dolphins were being taught. For instance, the word for "ball" was a white triangle. If the dolphin pressed its rostrum against the white triangle, the keyboard would generate a whistle and an assistant, hearing the distinctive whistle (in this case something like a wolf whistle) would get the dolphin a ball. The same went for "fish" (a white circle), and "rub" (a white "H"), and so on. The symbols would be moved around the keyboard to prevent the dolphin from simply memorizing a position on the keyboard.

Reiss took a different approach to such studies than many other scientists. While some researchers use hunger to motivate an animal to perform, Reiss's attitude in studying intelligence was, as she puts it, "to take a large-brained animal and encourage it to give its best stuff." This meant feeding the animals *before* they went to work. The approach produced results almost immediately.

The dolphins were taught to associate the white symbol with an object or activity (getting a rub or fish, e.g.), but they had to make the association with the whistle. After only nineteen sessions, the young male dolphins, Pan and Delphi, started mimicking the wolf whistle for "ball."

The way they learned the sound was interesting enough in itself. Reiss did spectrograms of both the whistles and the dolphins' response. The first thing they mimicked, says Reiss, was the end of the whistle. This seems to be similar to the way in which children learn to say long words. Then the dolphin would mimic the beginning of the whistle, and finally, the harmonics. Comparing the spectrographs, Reiss was astonished to see that the dolphin would do this reverse mimicry in the exact .6 second interval that was the length of the wolf whistle itself. In other words, within the span of the wolf whistle, the dolphin could reorder and replicate its elements. After a few tries, the dolphins would put the elements into their correct order and exactly mimic the sound. Try that sometime.

The study went well, providing additional data on the role of mimicry in vocal learning with dolphins. Perhaps the most interesting information to come out of this study, however, never made it into the paper Reiss and Brenda McCowan published in the *Journal of Comparative Psychology*. For instance, Pan, an eleven-month-old male, became so attached to the "fish" key, which would get him a herring or smelt, that Reiss had to take the key off since he was thinking of little else (the other young male, Delphi, preferred "rub" to fish, suggesting that young dolphins have individual preferences). The first day after the "fish" circle was removed, Pan came over and looked intently at the keyboard, as though he were looking for his favorite symbol. Not finding it, he went to the bottom of the pool, picked up a dropped piece of fish and then came back and placed it against an unused black key on the keyboard, perhaps thinking the omission was an oversight that he could correct.

Another bit of improvising that Reiss and McCowan left out of the published study was an incident that suggested that the dolphins were appropriating the whistles for their own use. At the end of the day Reiss would enlist the dolphins to clean up the pool by asking them to "fetch" various objects. Pan was happily earning fish in this manner one day, when, once again, Reiss gave him the "fetch" command. Scouring the pool he discovered that the only object left was the ball, and he could not retrieve it because it was in Delphi's mouth. Not about to be denied a fish, Pan went head to head with Delphi in a confrontation posture. What happened next was extraordinary.

Diana heard one of the dolphins give the "ball" whistle. Most likely it was Pan, because the whistle meant "give me the ball." She could not be sure, however, and thus never published the story.

There are other examples of dolphins appropriating as their own words and sounds introduced by humans. Sam Ridgway, one of the nation's leading experts on dolphin echolocation and the brain, recalls that some years back he and his colleagues would use a whistle as a "bridge" to reward the dolphins when they did something right. In effect, the whistle meant, "Attaboy!"

After using the whistle a number of times, Ridgway noticed that the dolphins had appropriated it themselves. Sometimes after they had performed flawlessly, the trainers would hear the whistle even though no one had blown theirs. Ridgway remarked that it was a little bit of self-congratulation—like the celebrations you see on television after a football player has scored a touchdown.

There is a world of difference between what a scientist can publish and what we encounter in the world. Far from carefully controlled procedures, there are many other examples of animals appropriating or expanding on words or signals they have learned from humans, some involving surprising animals. I always introduce stories about pets with a disclaimer because most are virtually impossible to verify. I'll offer a couple here, however, with all due caution.

Following a television interview in Atlanta, a woman came up to me and told me about her parents' dog. They had taught the animal to ring a bell beside the door when he wanted to go outside. They were quite proud of his achievement, at least until the dog began using the bell for his own purposes. His first innovation was to ring the bell when he wanted food. Instead of standing by the door while it was opened, he would go over to his food bowl and look up expectantly. Then he began ringing the bell when he just wanted attention.

I'm somewhat open to this story because I've had my own experiences with animals appropriating and generalizing a signal. When one of our Bengal cats, named Murghatroyd, was a kitten, he enjoyed getting into a wicker basket where we kept old magazines. We would pick up the basket and carry him around and he would get a lot of petting in the process. Murghy soon began using this as a signal that he wanted to be carried and petted. He would hop into the basket, catch a human's eye, and sit up in the posture he assumed when he wanted some attention.

When we moved from an apartment in New York City into a house up the Hudson River, the basket stayed behind. On the other hand, we did have a wooden log cradle that also had a handle, and Murghy soon began using the log carrier as a substitute for the wicker basket. When he first hopped in and looked at me I instantly knew what he wanted. The only problem was that Murghy had generous notions of human strength and forbearance and he would hop in whether there were logs in the cradle or not. I usually complied, however, considering the chore of carrying around twelve pounds of cat on top of thirty pounds of logs the price of maintaining a rare, direct channel of communication with the feline world.

Then Murghy introduced yet another innovation. I do most of my writing in the office behind the house. Murghy has decided that the office is his sanctuary from two stray kittens (now cats) that we adopted. The kittens worship Murghy, feelings that are not entirely reciprocated. Consequently, he comes out to the office whenever my wife and I are there, helping us work (which often involves wrestling my notes into submission, scattering them over the floor in the process), but mostly sleeping. Among the many objects in the office is a wicker tray with two handles on the sides. Sure enough, Murgy has designated this basket as his office sedan chair, and he will hop into it, assuming the same posture and giving me the same look that he has used with such success in the log carrier and the magazine holder.

Murghy's initial use of the magazine holder was probably the result of a simple association: Getting in yielded good results. The same type of thing could be done with almost any animal. Lou Garibaldi tells an amusing story about his tenure at the National Aquarium when he would occasionally have to bring VIPs around for private tours of the facility. The bigwigs liked to see the giant Pacific octopuses, but the octopuses liked to hide during the day. Lou's solution was to tell the keeper to rap twice on the glass of the tank every time he fed the octopus. Then, when Lou came by with visitors, he would simply rap twice on the glass and the octopus would come rocketing out, eager for an unscheduled meal (Lou says that he felt so guilty tricking the animal that he usually fed him, too).

What caught my attention about Murghy's appropriation of this message was the logical way in which he generalized. All his sedan chairs shared a few common characteristics: They were wood, they were rigid, they had a holding space, and they had some form of handle. Beyond that however, everything varied, from color to size to the shape of the basket. Moreover, Murghy never asked for a ride by jumping into a box, a canvas bag or a metal log holder. He seemed to recognize similarities between the objects, and perhaps "knew" that I would recognize the similarities. More to the point, it was not us humans who taught Murghy the general rules of cat portage (another easy task that could have been accomplished through operant conditioning), but Murghy who taught us. I shouldn't be surprised, I guess, since all of our cats give us very plain instructions, leading us repeatedly to cat bowls when they want to be fed, or to doors when they want to go out.

At the other end of the scale (at least in terms of size—as a cat, Murghy would never concede superiority to any other creature), Harry Peachey tells a story about an elephant that began helping out his keepers, prompting them to encourage this behavior though verbal commands, which the elephant then learned. Peachey says that the highly social elephants are predisposed to cooperate with humans if treated well, and Koko figured out when his keepers needed assistance separating and transferring the females in the group.

Ordinarily, when transferring a female, the keepers would yell to the elephant in question, "Connie transfer." Koko, an attentive listener, figured out what this meant. If Connie ignored the request, Koko would then intervene and guide her in the proper direction.

The keepers appreciated this help. After a while, if they asked Connie or one of the other elephants to transfer and got no response, they would then say, "Koko, give me a hand." Hearing this, Koko would step up and help.

After twenty-seven years of dealing with elephants, Harry Peachey is convinced that the animals understand the semantic content of some of the words they hear. They readily generalize, he notes, and he also believes that they will appropriate various elephant phrases when communicating with humans. "We had one Asian elephant female who would chirp and squeak when tickled," he says. "Later we realized that it was the same sound used when approached by a bull." In that case, however, the context of the sounds suggested that the chirps were signifying submissiveness—a different meaning than that implied by the happy occasion of a tickling session.

In recent years there has been a good deal of research into what goes on in the brain when we or an animal observe another doing a task. In the early 1990s, Vittorio Gallese and some colleagues at the University of Parma in Italy were recording the electrical activity in macaque brains. During their investigation they noticed that neurons in one part of the animal's premotor cortex would fire when the macaque watched an object being used in an action, but not when simply presented with the object itself. These same neurons, located in an area of the brain associated with sequences of movements, fired when an action was being performed or being observed. The discovery of these cells, dubbed "mirror neurons," got the attention of neurologists, cognitive scientists, and philosophers because it raised the possibility of a physical mechanism that could account for an animal's ability to understand the actions and moods of others.

Later, various brain-imaging studies on people showed a similar pattern of neuron-firing in an area of the brain similar in some ways to the area of the premotor cortex in monkeys. This discovery precipitated a whole new round of excitement because one of the areas, called Broca's Area, is active during speaking. Suddenly, scientists could see a mechanism in the brain that could prove useful not just in imitation and communication, but in understanding the intentions and state of mind of others, and even in empathy. It also showed a link between actions and language. The grammar of language might have been built on an ability to understand patterns of actions.

This is one more piece of evidence to suggest that before our ancestors developed spoken language they may have used some gestural form of communication. The fact that mirror neurons exist in varying forms of sophistication in other animals besides humans may explain their ability to decode human actions, as well as the ability of some animals to understand and generate utterances, sign language, or invented languages.

Philip Lieberman, a professor of cognitive and linguistic sciences at Brown, caused a stir in the early 1970s when he and a colleague proposed that Neanderthal (a cousin of *Homo sapiens* who disappeared roughly 30,000 years ago) could not generate the full range of sounds of modern humans, and that this gave a competitive advantage to Cro-Magnon man, who was more physically equipped for speech. He has been exploring the relationship between the brain, our physical structure, and the evolution of language ever since, and more recently he explored another aspect of language in his search to find the origins of language.

In 1993, Lieberman spent some time on the slopes of Mount Everest at the base camp that serves as the jump-off point for attempts on the summit. His purpose was to monitor the effects of high altitude on thinking and speech. What he discovered was that oxygen deprivation affected several parts of the brain in concert. As climbers started to slur their words and speech deteriorated, so did their judgment and other higher mental abilities. For Lieberman, this meant that motor control, speech, and thinking were inseparable.

Moreover, Lieberman argues that the adaptations involving control of the tongue, larynx, and lips when we talk are the evolutionary basis for complex human thought. In Lieberman's view, we can think because we can talk. Certainly something must account for the manifest difference in thinking ability between humans and any other great ape.

However, asserting that humans can think because they can speak does not necessarily mean that an animal that can't talk can't think, nor does it mean that any animal that can generate words can think. Lieberman notes that fine control of movements of the hands is one tributary to the development of language, and that ability is far more widely shared in apes than fine control of the ability to generate sounds. Orangutans have fine motor control over their lips and tongue but they lack the anatomy to generate vowels and consonants. There is a logic in the ability of motor control that is non-verbal, but clearly thinking nonetheless.

The easiest way to visualize this logic is to think of the way Tiger Woods prepares to play a par-five hole on a golf course. He will study the layout and then plan shots and choose the proper club accordingly. No words are necessary at any point while Mr. Woods is visualizing his attack on the course (unless the golfer seeks the advice of a caddy, but that's a different matter). Similarly, a chess grand master will visualize various scenarios, perhaps as many as five or six moves out, hypothetically exploring the implications of various moves until he or she envisions a set of moves that yields an advantage. Again, no words are necessary as the player lets the match unfold in his or her imagination.

In the case of chess, language does make it a lot easier to learn the rules of the game, but it is not essential. The point is that even without words we can replicate and manipulate models of the world, sometimes in quite sophisticated ways. One aspect of intelligence is that it allows us to weigh risks in the mind before taking action in the world. Clearly, language and the symbolic systems of mathematics and the other sciences give an enormous advantage when modeling reality, but it can be done with simpler symbolic systems or none at all. If other creatures use less elaborate representations than human language, it makes perfect sense that their technologies and communication might be less sophisticated, too, but they still might have tool-making and sophisticated communicative skills.

Consider this example from Borneo. Ann Russon recalls an incident in which a young orangutan resorted to mime to get what she felt was an obvious message across to a human. The female orang, named Siti, was nine at this point, and her dramatic story deserves a little background.

Siti had arrived at Wanarisit as a fifteen-month-old infant, and spent four years learning the ropes of being an orangutan and living in the forest before she was released into the Sungai

Wain protected area. Ann remembers her as one of her favorites, a bold young orangutan who would basically nominate other orangs to be her surrogate parents or mentors and would not take no for an answer. "You're my mom and you're my dad," was her attitude, says Ann, and amazingly, her chosen foster parents put up with it.

In any event, a good deal of this forest burned during the El Niño of 1998, and many orangutans, including Siti, disappeared. Ann feared she was dead. Then, in March 2000, Siti showed up, raiding a local garden on the edge of the forest. Instead of shooting the ape, the owner had the sense to call the staff at Wanarisit, who came and took Siti back to the facility.

She was quite thin and in very bad shape from her ordeal. After restoring her health, the staff again took her to the forest. This time, however, her progress was monitored by technicians who made sure that she had ample provisions until she got back up into the trees.

On the occasion in question, the little orangutan was trying to eat a coconut, an arduous process that involved chewing off the husk and then poking a finger through one of the "eyes" to get at the milk and meat. After chewing and poking through one eye, the little orang got tired and handed the coconut to an Indonesian technician named Nian. Russon was observing the scene and saw several split remains of coconut scattered around, suggesting that the assistant had cut open coconuts with his machete for the young orangutan on previous occasions.

This was a no-no, since the animals would not have access to room service in the wild. With Russon present, the assistant was not going to risk breaking the rules and sheepishly handed the coconut back to the young female. The young orang made another half-hearted try and then handed it back to the assistant. He handed it back to Siti.

Now the little orangutan was getting exasperated. Why wasn't this guy getting the message! So, instead of handing him the coconut immediately, she picked up a stick and, wielding it like a machete, smashed it down on top of the coconut in exact imitation of how a human would crack open a coconut with a machete. Then she handed the coconut back to the assistant, lest there was any doubt about what she wanted. Certainly, it would have been more efficient if the orangutan and the human shared a common language and she could simply tell him what she wanted, but even in the absence of words, she could be quite precise about what she wanted.

Apart from demonstrating Siti's ability to communicate her wants, Russon argues that this example also shows an ability to reflect on and alter her behavior to achieve a particular purpose. When simply handing over the coconut did not work, Siti sat back and figured out a way to alter the program to get the message across. As such it is another example of metacognition, and evidence of awareness.

Ann Russon notes that orangutans use actions to pass messages in the wild. For instance, if an orangutan has a history of aggression against another orang and then tries to approach in a more friendly manner, the other orangutan will back off, fearing attack. Once she observed an orangutan try such an approach several times, only to see the other orangutan back off. Finally, the formerly aggressive, but now friendly, orangutan tried to approach again, but quickly broke off his approach, turned to the side and pretended to feed. Since feeding is a higher priority than attack among orangutans, Russon felt that the message was, "Don't back off; see, I'm not going to attack you."

What about other forms of communication? There are many who believe that animals have other nonlinguistic ways of getting a message across. Cat people—those fascinated by felines big and small—in particular advance the notion that the animals are able to communicate by planting images or ideas in a person's head. I get approached regularly with stories of animal telepathy and prescience.

Penny Torres, who founded and runs the Oregon Tiger Sanctuary as a haven for big cats, tells two stories about Rajah, one of the sanctuary's Bengal tigers. After a huge four-foot snowfall one winter, Penny says that Rajah persistently "imaged" her to take him out (the most frequent description of cat communication is that the animals plant an image in a person's mind). As Penny took the big cat out, the roof collapsed. Had he not been moved, the building would have collapsed on him.

On another occasion, Penny asserts that Rajah "called" her into a meditation room. Once she entered the room, she noticed that a crystal placed there had so concentrated sunlight coming in the window that a cloth had started to burn. Without Rajah, says Torres, "we would never have discovered that in time." Any empiricist gets understandably nervous when such stories are raised, but, discounting the possibility that they are the product of an overheated imagination, they are worth considering.

There may be physical explanations for some examples of what appears like telepathy to us. I noted in *The Parrot's Lament* that what appeared to be ESP in the case of a parrot who would announce "Daddy's home" just minutes before Daddy would drive up the driveway might have been the bird's extraordinary sensitivity to vibration. The bird's owner would downshift at the bottom of a steep hill a block before arriving at home.

Our focus on sounds as a medium of communication might blind us to other channels. Harry Peachey points out that elephants can interpret and perhaps communicate a great deal through olfactory signals. In the animal's giant brain, olfactory lobes take up a good deal of space, permitting a sense of smell that might be one hundred times more sensitive than a

human's. Elephants may make extensive use of this rich channel in ways that we fail to notice. Just as dolphins may pick up
information that seems to us extrasensory because of their extraordinary sonar, elephants may be interpreting a whole
range of sensory information that is beyond the limits of our
senses.

Elephants also have access to parts of the sound spectrum
beyond human perception. They communicate by generating
ultra-low-frequency sounds, far below the range of sounds au-
dible to humans. Peachey says that if you stand in front of an
elephant generating these ultra-low-frequency sounds, you
don't hear it, but rather feel it as a distinct vibration in the ster-
num. Move to one side and the vibration vanishes, move back
in front of the elephant's head and it will reappear. "It's distinct," says Peachey, "like magic fingers."

Elephants will use this channel of communication to keep
everyone moving in the same direction, even though the herd
might be widely dispersed while foraging for food. Whales,
also highly social but wide-ranging animals, may use the extraordinary transmission properties of water to keep in touch
even when they are widely separated. More recently, some researchers have begun investigating whether tigers generate
ultra low frequency sounds that carry over great distances (if
proven, this might explain the highly social behaviors of an
animal that pursues a solitary career as a hunter).

Just because we cannot hear or see communication does not
require us to jump to telepathy as an explanation. On the other
hand, I've also had enough eerie experiences to make me wonder whether our tunnel-visioned obsession with syntax and se-
mantics obscures not only our view of how messages are
passed using human language, but whether we are somehow
ignoring entire channels through which messages are passed.

For instance, about three years ago, one of our cats disappeared. Her name is Samantha, but we call her Junior because she is the youngest of three Bengals we own. Junior is a pretty adventurous cat and when we moved to a river town north of New York City, she took it upon herself to become a feline Marco Polo.

Unfortunately, her dreams exceeded her grasp, or at least her feline skills, during her first months exploring the great outdoors. I spent a good deal of time rescuing her from trees or extracting her from garages before she developed some bush savvy. Whenever she was in trouble, however, she always told us where she was, either by yelling at the top of her lungs, or through some means I still don't understand.

In this case I was going out of town on a business trip, and by the time I left, Junior had already been gone for several days. Mary feared the worst. Between us we had walked virtually every street in the neighborhood calling her name until we were hoarse. We plastered the area with posters with pictures of her and where to call if she was found (after several disappearances we had a good supply of missing cat posters on hand).

More to reassure her than because I believed it was true, I told Mary, "You'd know it if she was dead. Just try to empty your mind and she will tell you where she is." To my absolute amazement, this is exactly what happened.

Driving back from New York City the following day, Mary suddenly got an image of a house in her head. She drove to a street a few blocks away (one that we had already canvassed), and parked in front of a house under construction. Sure enough, when she peered into the basement window, there was Junior with a bad case of laryngitis, but still trying to meow.

What are we to make of this? Obviously, we can't rule out that some logic was working in Mary's subconscious that was entirely separate from any messages that the desperate Junior was trying to send. It's also possible that Junior did send some infrasonic message that some part of Mary's brain recognized subconsciously. Some argue that tigers communicate through ultra-low frequencies: maybe little cats use some other range. No one knows where purring in cats comes from, so I suppose that they might be capable of sending signals beyond our range of hearing, but that we still sense.

I'm loath to rule out a physical explanation until all possibilities have been exhausted. But then, these inexplicable forms of communication also occur with humans who do not have particularly good hearing or special nerves for sensing vibration.

One fine Saturday in November I was driving my three-and-three-quarter-year-old son Alec to his twin cousins' birthday party in New York City. We were going to the Fire Department Museum on Spring Street in SoHo, and my route took us directly past the site of my regular poker game. Alec and I had been talking about a squash racket I had left in the back seat and as I approached the street where the game was hosted, I wondered whether I should tell Alec that this was where I played poker. I decided not to tell him because I did not want to get into a discussion of gambling with a three-year-old. So we continued down Washington Street in temporary silence. Just after we passed the street where I would have turned off for the game, Alec asked me, "Do you play poker with a squash racket?"

I was stunned. I started replaying the entire previous conversation to determine whether I might have muttered the word. But I hadn't. All the thoughts about poker had been in my head, and I had purposely chosen not to mention the game. The possibility that Alec might coincidentally decide to talk about poker was extremely remote. For diplomatic reasons I rarely mention poker at home since my wife's attitude toward the game is something less than wildly enthusiastic.

I cannot explain the seemingly telepathic communication

that sometimes surfaces between people and between animals and people, but it happens too frequently to be simply dismissed. Indeed, after the September 11, 2001, destruction of the World Trade Center, American intelligence agencies reactivated a program of drawing on "remote viewing" and other paranormal abilities in their search for Osama bin Laden and in attempts to predict future targets of terrorism. Hard-nosed materialists find this ludicrous, but the last word on what is material has yet to be written.

Perhaps there is some as yet unaccounted for physical mechanism that explains these occurrences without requiring that we throw cherished notions of reality out the window. Perhaps we feel people staring at us because they emit a faint chemical smell when concentrating. Just as we can smell fear, we might be able to smell hate, or a variety of other mental states.

Or perhaps we have to throw out cherished notions of reality. There is a physics that shows how influences affecting one object can simultaneously affect another, even if it's on the other side of the universe. The soft sciences mimic the paradigms of the hard sciences. Indeed, many of the absurdities of behaviorism, which sees all behavior including human behavior in terms of stimulus and rewards, derive from the attempt by psychologists to adapt their field to the physics of the early twentieth century. At the end of the twentieth century there is a nice symmetry between the model of words and their meanings discussed earlier, and the implied reality of quantum mechanics.

Unfortunately, this physics applies to the behavior of subatomic particles and not to objects in the visible world. Moreover, the set of equations that describe the behavior of these subatomic phenomena were never meant to be generalized into a model of reality. Rather, quantum mechanics was a set of mathematical principles developed by Werner Heisenberg and other physicists in the 1930s to describe the behavior of the invisible world of atomic particles. The predictions of quantum mechanics have passed every test, but the physics carries with it some implications that contradict our most cherished assumptions about the nature of matter. Among the most well-known aspects of quantum reality is the difficult-to-digest idea that if you isolate the position of a particle such as a photon you cannot know where it is going, while if you isolate its direction and movement you cannot know precisely where it is. In other words, light remains in some indeterminate state as the potential to be either wave or particle, until it is measured. Then, depending on how it is measured, it takes some particular form, but whichever form it takes, that form will not completely describe all aspects of light.

Quantum mechanics provides a possible way of accounting for the simultaneous appearance of thoughts in two minds without any communication. One experiment in particular has opened doors to this possibility, although it deals with the behavior of photons or electrons rather than thoughts. The experiment grew out of a thought experiment envisioned by Albert Einstein and two colleagues, Boris Podolsky and Nathan Rosen (ironically, Einstein pursued the thought experiment to highlight the absurdities of quantum mechanics; he never imagined that it could be done experimentally, and worse, verified).

To put this in layman's terms, one tenet of quantum mechanics implies that once subatomic objects such as photons from a common origin are linked in certain attributes (become entangled), they will remain correlated even if they are separated and travel in opposite directions. Change, for instance, the orientation of one photon, and its twin will instantly reorient even if it has traveled to the far corner of the universe. The idea gave Einstein heartburn because any such instant adjustment violates his principal of locality—the supposedly inviolable limit imposed by the speed of light.

Some years later physicists figured out how to actually test this proposition. The experiment involved emitting photons from a common light source, altering their polarization by running them through a field and then splitting the beam so that the photons head off in different directions. Once split, one beam is passed through another beam that subsequently alters its orientation, and simultaneously the other beam is measured to see whether it has changed as well. Starting with John Clauser and Abner Shimony this experiment has been tried in various forms more than a dozen times. Each time quantum mechanics has triumphed over common sense and Einstein's universal speed limit.

The path from photons to thought and remote viewing is tenuous at best, but it is worth pondering for no other reason than because it offers a possible physical explanation for phenomena that otherwise seem magical. If subatomic particles (which have parallel lives as wave functions) with a common origin remain correlated under certain influences, maybe consciousness does as well. The key word here is correlated. In quantum mechanics, the two photons do not communicate with each other; rather, they are correlated the way the different parts of a wave share symmetries.

The differences described by the words "correlate" and "communicate" in this context point to the utterly different realities of quantum mechanics and the familiar everyday world of classical physics, from which we draw our models of thought and language. Still, this idea has gained some momentum in recent years as scientists have postulated quantum entanglement for a growing number of particles. If the strange world of quantum mechanics does in fact account in some way for the entanglements of consciousness that we now consign to the realm of the paranormal, those explanations will require a complete and profound change in the ways in which linguists think about language and psychologists think about thought.

It is interesting that researchers looking to develop the next generation of computers are perfectly willing to do this, while theoreticians concerned with descriptions of language and thought still regard the implications of quantum mechanics as peripheral at best and lunatic at worst. The difference is between scientists who are interested in getting results and the more conservative climate of academia, where the risks of intellectual bravery greatly outweigh the rewards. Those studying communication and language might note that what is at the periphery of one paradigm turns out to be at the center of its successor.

Chapter Twelve

IT'S NOT WHAT YOU KNOW, IT'S WHO BELIEVES YOU

The Long and the Short of Intelligence

What is the purpose of intelligence? This is a very different question than "What is intelligence?" or "What produced it?" The obvious answer is that intelligence enhances the survival of a species, but if a jellyfish could talk, it might answer, "Not so fast, buddy." Humanity, the most intelligent species (by our own reckoning), has not been around long enough to make any assertions along those lines. Moreover, if the evolution of species were an industry and intelligence a business strategy, a hard-nosed CEO would look at the numbers and tell his managers to go back to the drawing board for a new plan.

As noted, the most successful species (at least until now) have been some of nature's dumbbells, like flatworms, jellyfish and sea turtles. We've been around as a species for maybe 200,000 years, and while we have taken over the planet, in the process we have been killing off or crowding out other species, poisoning the land and oceans, stripping the forests, altering the climate, and even fiddling with atmospheric mechanisms (such as the ozone layer and greenhouse gases) that permit life on earth. Are these the kinds of things a creature would do if that species were pursing a long-term strategy of survival?

Turn the question around, however, and ask whether these are the kinds of things a creature would do if it were pursing a short-term strategy, and the answer comes back a clarion yes! If an animal is not concerned with the long term, intelligence is a very useful ability to have. If a species needs to adapt to a changing environment, intelligence is an extremely useful ability to have. And if a species wants to flexibly alter the environment to enhance its short-term prospects, intelligence is absolutely crucial.

From a perspective that seeks immediate gain rather than long-term sustainability, the trade-offs that have marked human progress and economic development seem eminently reasonable, with one small catch. These trade-offs only work so long as there is some new landscape to alter once the old one has been exhausted. That's the rub: The short term eventually affects the long term.

Things that seem highly intelligent in the short term often prove to be incredibly stupid in retrospect. In their mad rush to modernize an agricultural economy, planners in the Soviet Union diverted the Amu Dar'ya and Syr Dar'ya rivers to irrigate cotton, rice, and other crops. Starved of its sources of water, the Aral Sea has shrunk to one fourth its original volume, changing the regional climate, killing off what was once one of the most productive fisheries in the world (supporting 60,000 jobs), and leaving behind a lifeless moonscape and diseased population that is proving far more costly than any of the profits reaped for a few years by collective farms. Costs to the economy run at about $6.5 billion annually, estimates of infant mortality run as high as a staggering eighteen percent, and the build-up of toxins and salts has made the region unfit for human habitation.

One would think that ecological nightmares like this would dissuade others from similar water diversion projects, but no, the short term rules. In Africa, Lake Chad has shrunk to one twentieth its size of just forty years ago because of overuse and diversions with similar effects; the Aswan Dam on the Nile has denied lower Egypt its annual replenishment of topsoil, beggaring agriculture and causing the entire Nile Delta to slowly sink and become inundated with salt water from the Mediterranean. There are plans, all highly thought through and intelligent, to divert the Okavango River to Namibia (which would starve the richest wetland in southern Africa), and a numbing number of other rivers.

Such projects may seem far afield in a book about stories of animal intelligence, but they loudly underscore what is often lost when scientists and philosophers turn their sights on the singular genius of humanity: Intelligence is not always intelligent. The projects mentioned above are huge, collective undertakings, pooling the intelligence and financial resources of many countries. Still, they will likely turn out to be dumb beyond all measure as their unintended consequences begin to surface over the years. The unrestrained use of intelligence can be self-destructive, to be sure, but it can also bring ecological chaos with it. Perhaps this is why nature doles out mental hardware so sparingly, and, even when it does endow a creature with some measure of intelligence, it also creates anatomical and cultural governors that act as controls on the ways in which intelligence can be put to use.

This is one way nature represents the long-term interests of a species even as evolution equips an animal with the brains to manipulate its world. I have been thinking about this idea ever since I noticed the degree to which a short attention span limited a chimp's ability to focus on the task at hand during sign language training. Typically, the chimp would concentrate for a few seconds and then break off to eat a reward, get a hug, or just burn off energy. It was for this reason that I was so intrigued with an experiment conducted by Sally Boysen, in which she would ask a chimp to pick between two trays with different amounts of M&Ms. If the chimp picked the larger tray, she would get the smaller tray while the larger amount would go to another chimp.

The chimp had to think smaller to get larger. The chimps could never do it when faced with actual M&Ms, but when tokens were substituted that weren't good to eat, the chimps figured out the answer almost immediately. In effect, the chimp's appetites were limiting its ability to deploy its reasoning ability, something that happens with human children, too, until they reach the age of four.

As a child matures, its brain develops the connections and structures to overrule its appetites. Once somewhat freed of physical controls, what acts as a limit on the way in which intelligence can be applied? Until extremely recently, the most plausible answer has been religion, customs, taboos, and other cultural restraints.

The late anthropologist Marvin Harris built his career on explaining cultural mores from this perspective. According to Harris, the Hindu ban on killing cows encoded a cost/benefit analysis that the cows were more valuable to farmers as a source of milk and to plow fields than as a one-time source of meat. While both Jews and Muslims won't eat pork because of the requirements of their religion, according to Harris, this ban guided ancient herders away from growing pigs that competed with humans for the same food sources and toward sheep and goats that can eat grasses impalatable to people and also provide milk, clothing, and pulling power. Indeed, these cultural constraints may be the device that enabled humans to develop such a large brain without killing ourselves off. Take away those cultural constraints and you get engineers who come up with projects to divert water from the Aral Sea, etc.

Not too long ago there was a contretemps in Connecticut precisely because a police chief recognized that there are occasions when intelligence is ill-suited for a particular job. The chief got in trouble for using IQ tests to screen *out* applicants who were too intelligent to be beat cops in his city. His argument was that a lot of police work involves monotonous waiting and repetition, and that putting a too-intelligent cop in that situation could be disruptive. As can be imagined, this reasoning was not greeted with wild enthusiasm by police unions and others, who resented the implication that being a cop was a job for dullards.

I noted in Chapter Two that the mutations that produce larger brains must be ubiquitous, meaning that a great variety of creatures have had a shot at developing larger brains, but, with few exceptions, it hasn't worked out. But it has certainly worked out with humans. While other brainy experiments likely ended up as roadkill on the highway of evolution, our ancestors got smarter and smarter. The largest-brained precursor to humanity did not always win the day (as evidenced by fossil remains of Neanderthal, who likely had a bigger brain than we do today), but the long-term trend has seen humanity develop a brain that dwarfs the size of our closest relatives.

For better and for worse, being intelligent has worked for us. Why? What we lump as intelligence likely arose because it enabled our ancestors to deal with change, quite probably a changing climate. Even if the big jump in intelligence had to do with managing an ever larger and more complex social system, the current theory *du jour*, the need for larger, complex groups was to some degree a response to ecological challenges.

There are striking correlations between periods of extreme climate upheaval and periods of rapid evolutionary change in our forebears. For instance, roughly 5.8 million years ago, during the era in which the first hominids split from the other great apes, climate was buffeted by a series of events including the Messinian salinity crisis. During this period sea level dropped to the point that the Mediterranean Sea was isolated from the Atlantic. As the huge body of water dried up, it left behind salts, while its evaporated waters fell as rainwater elsewhere, lowering the salinity of the oceans. With less salt, more of the oceans froze, setting in motion another cascade of climate changes, including cooling and drying in the African plains that are the supposed birthplace of our ancestral line.

This period lasted some 400,000 years, or roughly 20,000 hominid generations, a long tumultuous period during which a species adapted for a rapidly changing environment had a leg up on its competitors. The scale of the changes that occurred during this period is suggested by the great cascade that took place when the oceans rose to the point that waters reflooded the Mediterranean through Gilbraltar. According to Kenneth Hsu, one of the geophysicists who has studied this period, the ensuing flood ripped through the breached barrier at over one hundred miles per hour, creating a Gilbraltar waterfall one thousand times the volume of Niagara Falls, New York's fabled destination for honeymooners.

Since the Messinian crisis, periods of stability have been more the exception than the norm. When Panama rose from the oceans three million years ago, linking North and South America, it also interrupted circumequatorial currents and radically changed the way the sun's heat is distributed around the planet. Some argue that this event set in motion the formation of the polar ice caps and a series of ice ages, events that also had great bearing on human evolution. The past million years or so, a period that has seen fifteen major ice ages, was also a period of evolutionary ferment. *Australopithecus robustus* died out in the middle of the reign of *Homo erectus*. In this most recent period of extreme climatic upheaval, *Homo erectus* was supplanted by *Homo sapiens* (and then by *Homo sapiens sapiens*), while Neanderthal had its brief, 170,000-year reign (although any condescension on our part is premature, since this is about the time that we have been on the planet).

Naturally, every other surviving species on earth also contended with these wild climatic swings, and many of them managed to survive without becoming markedly more intelligent. Those species that have enormous numbers of offspring (called R-Strategists by biologists) play the odds that some of their offspring will be adapted for the changed world. Those animals that have fewer offspring and invest a lot in their rearing (called K-strategists), tend to fare less well during periods of rapid change. No less than four Australopithecus lines (and probably a few more that have yet to be discovered) have died out since we split from our common, chimplike ancestor. So did four members of the Homo line.

Given the possible role of climate change in the rise and fall of every one of our ancestors, I find it somewhat ironic that we are now changing the climate ourselves. The track record of climate as an effective eraser of hominids (and during historical times, as an eraser of civilizations) should at least give us pause. There is a bit of cosmic humor in the possibility that an intelligence spurred in part by the effects of climate change might change climate in ways that threatens the survival of earth's most intelligent creature.

While there will always be disagreements about its origins, one thing is clear. Intelligence did not arise to enable Michelangelo to paint the ceiling of the Sistine Chapel or Beethoven to compose the *Emperor's Concerto*, or to enable Darwin to first articulate how species evolve. These signal acts of genius may define for us the essence of humanity, but they were all byproducts of a natural ability that had utilitarian roots. It's important to keep this in mind when thinking about intelligence and whether other creatures might possess higher mental abilities.

It may be hard to get an animal started on the road to intelligence as we variously define it, but once this adaptation attains some traction it does seem to gain momentum. Perhaps there is some positive feedback, but using brainpower to find fruit, or search for buried tubers, or understand a dynamic and complex social structure has to be adaptive every step of the way or that line will die out. There could be some tipping point beyond which a species has such an investment in the behavioral flexibility permitted by higher mental abilities that only the brainier survive when confronted with rapid environmental change.

Homo habilus had a brain thirty percent larger than his predecessor, Australopithecus, and very likely that extra cognitive horsepower gave this direct ancestor a competitive advantage, since Australopithecus died out (although this line had a very good run, with some species lasting well over one million years). *Homo erectus*, with a fifty percent larger brain than *Homo habilus*, was better equipped to adapt to whatever curveballs nature threw in terms of climate change and other events. *Homo erectus* had a very long run, too, until we came along. The *Homo erectus* brain was very nearly the size of ours, with the exception that its neo-cortex was only two-thirds the size of that of a modern *Homo sapiens*.

At each stage, added brainpower gave us an edge, and as that additional brain size grabbed a bigger piece of our metabolic budget, it also made us more dependent on brains. The evolutionary lesson seems to be that if you are going to be smart, you'd better keep getting smarter.

At least that seems to be the lesson if we use *Homo sapiens sapiens* as our measuring stick. I have very little doubt that even the most formidable modern human could not hold his own in a physical contest with an ordinary Joe *Homo erectus*. Just as clearly, *Homo erectus* would not stand a chance against humans with our weapons and ability to strategize. Through our brains and our ability to pool our intelligence, we have, in effect, rebuilt the shell that the octopus lost.

So intelligence is short-term, imperfect, incomplete, and probably addictive, but what is it? Nobody agrees, although there are many persuasive arguments. A stack of books and papers written on this subject down through the years would reach to the moon. Rather than revisit yet another interminable debate, I thought I'd keep the focus on what intelligence does. With no scientific consensus to guide us, that is all we can do anyway.

In the simplest sense, intelligence allows an animal to integrate the information of the senses into patterns and then enables an interpretation of those patterns to predict and explain events beyond the constraints of immediate experience and time. The more intelligent the animal, the more elaborate, the richer and more useful the model can be. If an animal develops the ability to symbolically represent observations and the rules that link those observations into patterns, better yet. Better still if evolution equips it with a means of communicating its analysis and predictions to others so that the collective intelligence of a group can be brought to bear on a problem. If this system of communication involves spoken words and a grammar, terrific, but if it involves some other way of drawing on the wisdom of others, that works, too.

As noted in the previous chapter, some argue that animals including cats, big and small, achieve what we accomplish through language through some form of telepathy such as imaging or shared vision, in which we literally see the real or imagined through another's eyes. Keeping in mind that no one has as yet come up with a plausible explanation about how such a facility might work in physical terms, I'm still open to this possibility. There are enough mysteries in human perception, such as knowing when someone is staring at you, that it is entirely possible that some new paradigm of perception inclusive of telepathy might emerge someday. Whether or not powers such as shared vision are real or a paranormal fantasy, it is important to remind ourselves that science is by its nature incomplete. While it is highly unlikely that some alternative system as rich and productive as language and symbolic thought has evolved in other species, nature may well have experimented with other strategies.

However it is achieved, the pooling and leveraging of knowledge is perhaps the most important development in the evolution of higher mental abilities. Strip one person of his weapons and tools, and he or she might figure out a way to build a shelter, mount a defense against threats, and find food. Put fifty people without tools and weapons in virtually any ecosystem on earth and there is little question that most would find a way to survive, even in some of the most inhospitable places on earth. Chances are the group would very quickly figure out some division of labor. If they found themselves in a riverine or marine environment they would figure out how to catch fish and find mollusks. If they were dropped into the Serengeti they would hunt wildebeest.

This is the kernel of truth underlying those ludicrous reality-based survival shows that have enjoyed a brief vogue in recent years. We are fascinated because we can go along in our imaginations, envisioning how we would deal with the physical and social challenges facing the individuals and the group. There is also a kernel of truth in the shows' emphasis on social skills as a survival skill. Not for nothing did the most Machiavellian member of the first *Survivor* series end up the last man standing.

As long as we are referring to television, another newly popular genre also captures the collective genius of humanity (television executives are highly skilled at ferreting out archetypal desires and anxieties in the American psyche). These are the "Junkyard Wars" competitions in which teams of engineers are given the challenge of building a vehicle to perform some task using only the materials they can scavenge from a scrap heap. The task might be to climb a wall and then traverse a river. The key to success is teamwork, but also skillful trading skills if a team is to secure some useful piece of trash coveted by more than one group.

While we are on the subject of games, it merits a brief digression to discuss one human amusement that, to my mind, reflects the evolutionary roots of intelligence. This is the card game poker, in which success involves quantitative skills to be sure, but also mind reading, deception, emotional intelligence, and other social skills, all factors that humans draw on when they compete and cooperate in group situations. Then when I go off for my weekly poker game I can rationalize this indulgence as an expression of the genius of one species.

The prospects of a human individual increase with the size of the group he or she is affiliated with when confronted by novel circumstances. This works at the conscious level as we draw on the knowledge and experience of others, but it also seems to work on an unconscious level as well. Drop people into an office, and they will perform better on the same task than they will perform individually on the same problem. This was the result of research done by economists Alan Blinder and John Morgan at Princeton University. Beyond pooling information, merely being in close proximity to other humans working on the same problem seems to enhance our problem-solving abilities.

The same is not true of most other species. A leopard, perhaps nature's perfect predator, is highly adaptable and might survive in a wide variety of environments, but the chances of an individual leopard would decrease, not increase, if the animal were part of a group of fifty dropped into northern Canada. Chimpanzees do far better in a group than alone, and a group of chimpanzees dropped into Yellowstone Park might do better than an individual, but it would not do as well as a group of humans.

The great advances in civilization, from the advent of markets to irrigation to sanitation systems, have all been collective efforts involving the integration of both labor and intelligence. The larger the pool of brains that can be tapped or networked, the more knowledge gained.

While the hunter-gatherer of 50,000 years ago might have equivalent brainpower to anyone today, we have the inestimable advantage of being able to draw on the accrued lessons of millions of minds and, depending on the problem, the brainpower and expertise of thousands, if not millions, of people. The crucial element that allows us to draw on this intelligence is the network of social bonds that allow us to trust information and its source, and it is easy to forget that the nature of such networks has not materially changed since human society first took shape.

Today, humanity enjoys the fruits of living in what has been called the Information Age, meaning that computers and telecommunications enable us to process, store, and disseminate information that enhances our security, health, prosperity, and cultural life. I would argue that this designation points to a vast misconception of the key ingredient in human material progress. For one thing, information only becomes useful once it has been put in context, in the form of knowledge. Equally important, knowledge is only as useful as the degree to which it is accepted as knowledge by others.

In other words, the certification and communication of information eclipses the value of the information itself. Once humanity began to gather in large groups and specialize, the history of technology, from the invention of granaries to the nuclear arms race, is the history of innovations that serve the defense, feeding, and integuments that support ever larger groups. Today the clear success of the Internet is e-mail, through which hundreds of millions of users send some eight billion messages a day. But e-mail simply leverages existing relationships the way the telephone did seventy-five years ago, and ritual greetings have done since prehistory for nomadic peoples. What holds a group together? Relationships. And what holds relationships together? Trust, need, and mutual understanding.

Here then is a point where intelligence, social groups, and communication converge. Someone might have developed a perpetual motion machine or found some infinite and nonpolluting new source of energy, or the fabled carburetor that quadruples automobile mileage. These discoveries, however, will only have any meaning if others besides their inventor believe in them. An Afghani woman might discover the cure for cancer, but if she has the misfortune to live in areas controlled by the Taliban, her discovery will never see the light of day.

Intelligence is only as good as its expression, and is limited not just by the language used to disseminate discoveries or insights but by the credibility of whoever does the disseminating. Intelligence is as intelligence does, and its potential application is limited by noncognitive social factors such as kinship, trust, position in the group, and the ability to reach an understanding on the meaning of terms. We see all these social factors at work in a host of animals. This is one of the fascinating aspects of the Kibale chimps and their experiments with weapons. Imoso is relatively young, but he is also the dominant male. Did his position as alpha male ratify this new behavior in any way, and influence Johnny's decision to try beating a female with a stick? In any event, in both humans and animals the innovations are validated in a social matrix. Here is something we share with other creatures, whether or not we acknowledge continuity in higher mental abilities.

Chapter Thirteen

CONVERGENCE, EMERGENCE, AND BEYOND

Conclusion

Once again I'm looking at squirrels outside my window. First it was freezing with few breaks following Christmas and then unseasonably warm, vindicating to some degree the opposite predictions of the woolly bear caterpillars and the oak trees, but also providing ammunition for the critics of folk wisdom. Once again I am struck by the way in which nature optimized squirrels for life in the trees, and how this design has been used and reused through the eons by squirrels, monkeys, and other mammals. My thoughts turn to other examples of convergent evolution. For instance, pangolins and anteaters look alike except for the pangolins' scaly skin. They both have elongated snouts and powerful forelegs with big claws designed for digging. Despite these similarities, they are from entirely different mammalian orders, as distantly related as primates and pigs. The similarities are the result of nature optimizing the design for an animal that digs for insects.

I find the notion of convergent evolution quite arresting. On the one hand it implies that if an optimum design exists to exploit certain ecological niches, nature can converge on that design from many different directions. Convergent evolution suggests that in some cases what you do or where you live has more to do with determining your shape and abilities than who your ancestors were. Paleontologists have found the fossil remains of a five-million-year-old dolphin dubbed "Obobeno-cetops" that had tusks very similar to those of a walrus; nature has apparently decided that these swept-back tusks are the best design for a mollusk eater.

If convergent evolution applies to physical characteristics, might it not also apply to cognitive abilities?

Consider the dolphin, which has demonstrated some ability to understand words, the hierarchical importance of word order in commands, and other abstract concepts despite the fact that its brain structure is dramatically different from that of a human or primate. Instead of a neo-cortex, the dolphin has orbital lobes. The dolphin brain has more cortical folding (an organization that permits greater surface area in the human neo-cortex) than its human counterpart, but it is thinner than a human's. Laurie Merino, a leading psychobiologist studying the dolphin brain at Emory University in Atlanta, suggests that it is possible that the processing power associated with volume and thickness in human brains might be partially achieved through increased surface area in a dolphin. Radically different paths, but they converge in permitting self-recognition, some capacity for analysis, and perhaps self-awareness.

This is not to say that all smart creatures think alike—the differences in the way in which a dolphin or a human or a predator or an herbivore perceive the world would have powerful effects on the mental landscape. Rather, it is to suggest that perhaps there are different paths to certain common higher mental abilities that are then colored by the life history of the animal in question.

Try to put yourself in the mind of a hunter-gatherer in the Borneo rain forest. It is difficult, but it is possible because we share abilities, longings, and other emotions even if our lives are utterly different. Then jump back in time to the dawn of the species and try to jump to the mind of *Homo erectus*. Stepping on mental stones from there, hop to Australopithecus, and from there to our common chimplike ancestor. Throughout that journey certain elements will remain the same.

This technique does not work when we try to imagine the common elements we share with the mental life of a dolphin. Their environment is so utterly different that the mind simply reels. On the other hand, despite our alien worlds, we share much in common with dolphins, including a highly complex social structure. The optimized design in the mental realm—the mental equivalent of the elongated snouts and powerful forelegs of pangolins—might be an ability that permits budding Machiavellis to analyze social dynamics. Many species depend on the ability to deceive. Given enough time, nature can encode deceptions at the genetic level in the very shape and look of an animal, creating a sea horse that looks like seaweed. It can also encode behavioral deceptions at the genetic level, such as the zone-tailed hawk, a species that mimics the flight pattern of a harmless vulture to get past the early warning systems of its prey. But then, in complex social groups, where improvisational deception is important, nature has created a facility to create deceptions on the spot.

The best deceivers are those who can put themselves into the minds of those they would manipulate, and that ability emerged as well (possibly as a result of these selective pressures or possibly in response to other factors) in humans and probably a few other animals. Dolphin networkers and human networkers may think alike in certain respects, even if these abilities were enabled by entirely different brain structures. If true, cognitive convergent evolution would speak eloquently about the way evolution opportunistically exploits whatever is at hand as animals adapt to change.

Certainly, the notion of convergent evolution in the cognitive sphere would help us understand why the orangutan, likely a more distant relative than the chimp or gorilla, would seem more humanlike in form and thought processes than any other great ape.

There is another concept that helps us understand the orangutan and, ultimately, offers a suggestion about the answer to the riddle of the octopus. This is the idea of emergence. I like the idea that in language meanings are emergent, as context and conversation gradually define meanings. In this sense, and in the sense that intelligence is expressed in a social setting, knowledge is emergent as well, and bound up with communication. If intelligence is as intelligence does, then it is limited by the richness and openness of the representational system that allows the transmission of its products as well as the openness of the social situation that validates its products.

All of this would seem to leave the solitary octopus and the relatively solitary orangutan out in the cold (although, as Ann Russon points out, orangutan life may be characterized by more complex social interactions than has been previously supposed). There is, however, another sense in which an ability can be emergent.

To thrive in its highly variable environment as a hunter, the octopus must have very flexible control over the use of its eight arms, and also an opportunistic ability to innovate on the spot (much as Mather and Anderson demonstrated when creating hurdles that prevented octopuses from getting at various mollusks). The neural equipment that permits this might have the side benefit of some capacity for analysis and observational learning that emerges or becomes evident in captivity. Perhaps what equips an octopus for life in the wild also equips it to learn to deal with humans in extraordinary circumstances. Perhaps interactions with humans elicit a particular form and give a particular shape to abilities that might be differently expressed in the wild.

After all, we have arbitrarily set the terms for how we will look for intelligence. We have defined it a certain way, and look for abilities to represent and create patterns, evidence of self-awareness, theories of mind, metacognition, and all the other touchstones of our view of the cognitive landscape. To the degree that selective pressures converge to produce a particular result, we may find these attributors to varying degrees. In other cases, we might elicit an ability in a creature that has the capacity to demonstrate what we are looking for, but that might use that capacity in entirely different ways in the wild. But then, we might be missing whole different worlds of thinking and communicating because we see what we want to see and assume that what we see is reality. The world, however, may be enriched and quickened by far more minds that we have yet imagined.

INDEX

ABOUT THE AUTHOR

Eugene Linden is an award-winning journalist and the author of *The Parrot's Lament, The Future in Plain Sight, Silent Partners,* and other books on animals and the environment. He has consulted for the US State Department, the United Nations Development Program, and he is a widely traveled speaker and lecturer. In 2001, Yale University named him a Poynter Fellow in recognition of his writing on the environment. He lives in Nyack, New York.